The New Americans
Recent Immigration and American Society

Edited by
Steven J. Gold and Rubén G. Rumbaut

A Series from LFB Scholarly

Hispanic Immigrant Identity
Political Allegiance vs. Cultural Preference

George I. Monsivais

LFB Scholarly Publishing LLC
New York 2004

56085625

Library of Congress Cataloging-in-Publication Data

Monsivais, George I., 1956-
 Hispanic immigrant identity : political allegiance vs. cultural
preference / George I. Monsivais.
   p. cm. -- (The new Americans)
 Includes bibliographical references and index.
 ISBN 1-59332-065-5 (alk. paper)
  1. Hispanic Americans--Ethnic identity. 2. Immigrants--United
States--Social conditions. 3. Hispanic Americans--Politics and
government. 4. Immigrants--United States--Political activity. 5.
Allegiance--United States. 6. National characteristics, American.
 I. Title. II. Series: New Americans (LFB Scholarly Publishing LLC)
  E184.S75M654 2004
  305.868'073--dc22

2004016950

ISBN 1-59332-065-5

Printed on acid-free 250-year-life paper.

Manufactured in the United States of America.

To my Family

To my Friends

To my Homeland

To my People

To my God

Table of Contents

Introduction.. 1

What is an American?... 13

Logistic Analysis of the Allegiance Variable 81

Talking to the People: The Focus Groups........................... 103

Conclusions.. 129

Footnotes... 137

Bibliography 147

Index 157

FOREWORD

In 1995, while conducting focus group with Hispanic immigrants, I uncovered a paradox between the social/political behavior and the national self-identification of many of participants. Some participants expressed strong desires to live in the United States and be involved in their local communities, however, they self-identified with their countries of origin and had no intentions of becoming "American." The National Latino Immigrant Survey as reported in *New Americans by Choice* (Pachon and DeSipio, 1994) had similar findings with nearly half (49.5%) of the participants (all legal residents) self-identifying with their countries of origin.

One question raised by these findings was whether Hispanic immigrants self-identifying with their countries of origin were expressing political allegiance or merely expressing cultural preference. Prior experience with this population suggested that in all likelihood, they were not making declarative political statements, but rather only expressing cultural preference. If this were the case, one would expect that criteria defining what it is to be an American would not adequately predict whether a respondent would self-identify as an American or with their country of origin.

The research described in this book used a three-step approach to examine this question. First, some minimum criteria of being "American" were developed through an examination of relevant historical and current literature and Supreme Court decisions. Next, a secondary analysis of the NLIS data examined the relationship between the developed criteria and the NLIS respondents' national self-identification. Lastly, focus group interviews were conducted with legal Hispanic immigrants exploring what they meant when they self-identified as Americans or with their countries of origin.

The literature review developed four points as a minimum criteria defining being American: 1) belief in the American system of government, 2) participation in voluntary organizations, 3) participation in the political/electoral process, and 4) learning English sufficient to be able to participate in the political process. The secondary analysis of the NLIS data revealed that when operationalized through variables in the NLIS, most of the criteria did not predict national self-identification among NLIS respondents. The focus groups results showed that overall, when participants identified themselves as American or with their countries of origin; they were expressing ethnic/racial or cultural concepts, and not political preferences.

Acknowledgements

Most worth while human endeavors are not accomplished alone. If this particular endeavor is worthwhile at all, it is due in great part to the bounteous assistance and support received from so many individuals. I will here express appreciation to those who guided me through the this work: Dr. Harry Pachon, Dr. Gary Segura, Dr. Jean Schroedel, and Dr. Douglas Hooper.

CHAPTER 1

Introduction

In January of 1995, while conducting group interviews in Miami, Florida, with immigrants from Central America, South America, and Cuba, I discovered modest evidence of an apparent paradox between the social/political behavior and the expressed national allegiance of some of the participants. Although the principal focus of the group interviews was not to discuss politics or political behavior, part of the interviews revolved around:

- how the individuals had come to the United States,

- how long they had been in the United States,

- their general attitudes about living in the United States, and

- their general attitudes about interacting with the resident Anglo population.

It was in this setting, that I observed an apparent paradox in that although some of the participants in the groups:

- had legally immigrated to the U.S.,

- Were very appreciative of being in the U.S.,

- continued in the U.S. as legal residents, or had obtained U.S. citizenship,

- considered living conditions in the U.S. better than living condition in their countries of origin,

- expressed a desire to be part of and improve their local communities, and

- expressed a desire to participate in or related a history of having participated politically in the U.S.,

nevertheless they self-identified with their countries of origin and did not view themselves as, nor had any intentions of becoming, in their words, "American."[1]

Several months later, I conducted additional interviews in the Houston, Texas, area. The participants in these groups were principally immigrants from Mexico and Central America with a few individuals of Mexican heritage born in the U.S. As in Miami, many of the participants were legal immigrants who were either residing in the U.S. legally, or who had obtained U.S. citizenship. During the course of these interviews, respondents expressed attitudes similar to those observed in Miami, and as in Miami, some of the individuals in the Houston interview groups self-identified with their countries of origin and noted they did not consider themselves "American."

These group interview participants in Miami and Houston presented the following apparent paradoxical situation. They:

- were individuals who legally immigrated to the United States,

- were thankful to be in the United States,

- maintained legal residency or had obtained U.S. citizenship,

- participated in community affairs, but

- nevertheless continued to self-identify with their countries of origin rather than with the United States.

Although group interview participants in both Miami and Houston had manifested the same paradox, participants for these group interviews had not been drawn from, and therefore possibly did not represent the general Hispanic population. Therefore, although some of the participants in these groups had served as an excellent initial example of the paradox in question, unless this paradox was seen manifest in a broader more representative sample of Hispanic immigrants, these initial observations might merely be as curious anomalies.

A brief search revealed that this paradox did in fact exist in a very broad and representative sample of Hispanic immigrants: the National Latino Immigrant Survey (NLIS) conducted in 1988 and reported in *New Americans by Choice* (Pachon and DeSipio, 1994). Participants in this study were 1) all legal Hispanic immigrants, who 2) had been in the United States for five or more years. Respondent to the NLIS were asked:

Which of the following best describes how you see yourself:

> *More as an American,*
> *More as a member of your home country, or*
> *As something else?*

The results of the unweighted sample were as follows:

More as an American	*42.6%*
More as a member of your home country	*49.5%*
As something else	*7.9%*

Using the weighting scheme developed by the authors yielded the following results:

More as an American	*38%*
More as a member of your home country	*54%*
As something else	*8%*

By either measure, approximately half of the respondents to the NLIS appear to manifest at least some of the same paradoxical behavior observed in the Miami and Houston interviews, namely they are legal immigrants to the U.S., expressing a form of desire to reside in the U.S. by having been here for at least five years, performing the affirmative action of fulfilling the requirements to maintain legal residence or even obtain citizenship, but nevertheless self-identifying with their countries of origin rather than with the United States.

Why This Is an Issue of Importance

Why should this apparent paradox be explored and better understood? As of the 2000 Census, Hispanics constitute the largest minority group in the United States.[2] According to estimates released by the Census Bureau published in September 2003, Hispanics comprise over 34% of the population in the two most populous states, California and Texas, and over 13% of the population in the next three most populous states, New York (16%), Florida (18%), and Illinois (13%).[3] New Mexico boasts the highest percent Hispanic population (43%). Although certainly not all of the Hispanics in these states are immigrants, Hispanic immigrants do comprise the largest proportion of immigrants into the United States in recent years.[4] Census Bureau estimates in 2002 were that Latin Americans were 52% of all foreign-born residents in the U.S.[5] All these figures point to the fact that the population involved in this paradox, the population of interest, continues to grow.

While this immigrant population continues to grow at a rapid pace, "anti-immigrant sentiment, as expressed in public opinion polls, legislative initiatives and media reports, reached a post-World War II peak in the mid-1990's" (Muller 1997, 105). The terrorist attacks of September 11, 2001 roused additional anti-immigrant feelings.[6]

Leo R. Chavez notes that, a principal concern regarding new immigrants is their non-assimilation into American culture.

> The new immigrants are *trans*nationalists [emphasis in original], or people who maintain social linkages back in the home country; they are not bound by national borders and their multiple identities are situated in communities that cross nations. Transnational migrants threaten a singular vision of the nation because they

allegedly bring multiculturalism' and not assimilation.
(Chavez 1997, 62)

The results reported above from respondents to the NLIS could be interpreted as evidence that many legal Hispanic immigrants are "transnationals." If this is the case, and one further assumes that transnationals do in fact threaten the nation by encouraging multiculturalism rather than assimilation, then one might conclude that a threat is posed to the "singular vision" of the nation by legal Hispanic immigrants.

The growth of the population of interest in combination with continuing anti-immigrant feelings by large segments of the population make the examination of this apparent paradox particularly salient at this time. That these current feelings are merely the latest manifestation of anti-immigrant feelings dating back to before the Revolutionary War[7] does not make the issues or this apparent paradox any less interesting, but rather it demonstrates the enduring nature of the issue, and the historic and continuing concern regarding the impact of immigrants on the United States.[8]

Research Question and Hypothesis

The paradox noted above could be restated as follows:

> Some Hispanic immigrants who manifest social and political behavior which would lead one to believe they would self-identify themselves as "American," in fact self-identify with their countries of origin.

The apparent mismatch between the behavior of these immigrants and their stated self-identification with their countries of origin is caused by two factors. First, because their behaviors to some degree appear to typify "American" values (obedience to the law, appreciation for the life in America, civic participation, etc.), and second, the assumption that their statements of self-identification with their countries of origin are somehow political in nature.

But what if their statements were not political in nature, but rather statements of cultural preference? This would resolve the apparent paradox. In fact, there is reason to believe that a cultural rather than a political statement is what some of the participants in the focus groups intended.

In the focus group interviews where the apparent paradox was initially observed, the respondents were expressing self-identification with their countries of origin using phrases such as, "Yo soy Cubano," or "Chileno" or "Colombiano" to express this identity. The fact that they identified themselves as "Cubano," "Chileno," or "Colombiano" rather than as "Hispano" or "Latino" indicated a connection to their country of origin, not just to a broad Hispanic or Latino cultural heritage.[9] On first hearing such comments, most observers might conclude that the respondents were stating expressions of national allegiance, with its associated political connotations. However, it must be remembered that the context of these focus groups dealt with cultural issues. This broader context to the statements raises the question as to whether the expressions were truly affirmations of political identification or whether they were expressions of cultural preference.

The confusion of what was intended by these statements is illustrated by the additional observation of how some parents among the focus group respondents described being American. More than one parent respondent expressed concern about their children becoming Americanized which they defined as watching lots of television, playing video games all day, and being disrespectful to parents and other adults. As they described it, having their children remain "Mexican" ("Cubano," "Chileno," or "Colombiano") meant maintaining the old country values of respect, family togetherness, and hard work.

Thus, in these cases, although the statements of national identity made by these parent respondents initially appeared to be political, the additional context they provided in their statements show the statements to be expressions of cultural preference.

These and other observations led to this hypothesis:

> There is no relationship between a legal Hispanic immigrant's belief in and adherence to criteria which we consider to be defining of what it means to be "American" and that immigrant's self-identification with the U.S. or their country of origin.

If this is true, we should expect to find that when placed in a statistical model the attributes which we consider as defining what it means to be an American do not predict an immigrant's self-identification with the U.S. or with their country of origin. Further, we would expect that if respondents were given the opportunity to explain their choice of identifying with their countries of origin rather than with the U.S., they would express their selection more in terms of social or cultural factors than in expressions of political allegiances.

Approach

The research described in this book tested this hypothesis using a three-step approach. First, a minimum criteria was developed describing what it means to be an American. This was done through an examination of relevant literature and United States Supreme Court cases. Next, a secondary analysis of the NLIS data was conducted to examine the relationship between the developed minimum criteria and the NLIS respondents' national self-identification (American or country of origin). Lastly, focus group interviews were conducted to explore more deeply with groups of legal Hispanic immigrants what they mean when they identify themselves as Americans or with their countries of origin. Each of these approaches will now be discussed in greater detail.

Developing Minimum Criteria of What it Means to Be an American

As described above, people seem to have a concept, although often unarticulated, of what it means to be American. Samuel P. Huntington, in his book *American Politics: The Promise of Disharmony* observed that:

> People have been attempting to define American national identity or "national character" ever since national consciousness first emerged in the eighteenth

century. Personality traits, social characteristics,
geographic and environmental features, behavioral
patterns, and historical experiences have all been
invoked by one analyst or another. (Huntington 1981,
13)

To develop an absolute definition of an American creed or the
American national identity is beyond the scope of this examination. The
objective here is only to identify criteria which will represent a minimum
threshold of what it means to be an American. If at this minimum
threshold differences can be observed between those who identify
themselves as Americans and those who identify with their countries of
origin, then it would be reasonably inferred that those differences would
exist under more stringent criteria.

A list of core duties, values, beliefs, or behaviors which constitute the
minimum threshold of being an American will be developed by examining
historical and current attitudes toward immigrants as found in historical
writings, current popular commentaries, and the relevant academic
literature. Further, Supreme Court decisions addressing who qualifies for
full participation and legal acknowledgment as an "American" will be
used to demonstrate the changes in legal opinions over time as to who
qualifies as an American, and ultimately what criteria are now legally
unacceptable for disqualifying someone from receiving full legal
consideration as an American. Criteria determined by the Court to be
legally unacceptable would similarly be unacceptable for a minimum
threshold of what it means to be American. Therefore, examining the
criteria the Court has deemed as unacceptable and eliminating those
criteria from consideration will assist in creating this minimum threshold
definition.

Quantitative Analysis of the NLIS Data

Once minimum threshold criteria for a definition of what it means to be an
American have been developed, variables will be selected from the NLIS
to operationalize those criteria. Because the NLIS was not specifically
designed to examine the issue of national self-identification, only a subset
of variables from the NLIS will be selected to operationalize the criteria.

Where possible, a set of variables from the NLIS will be combined into a summary scale in order to create a single indicator variable for a criterion. For example, if political participation were defined as one of the minimum criteria defining what it mean to be an American, the several variables in the NLIS dealing with political participation would be combined into a summary scale to provide a single value of political participation for each respondent. Appropriate statistical measures (e.g. scale reliability and factor analysis) will be used to ensure that the combination of the different variables into a summary scale is appropriate.

After the NLIS variables are selected, and the summary variables are constructed, those variables, along with appropriate control variables (age, sex, income, etc.), will be used in a logistic regression model to examine the predictive ability of the criteria developed through the literature review in predicting whether NLIS respondents would identify themselves as American or with their countries of origin. Logistic regression is an appropriate statistical method to use in this case because the variable being examined, national self-identification, will be treated as a dichotomous variable: those who identify themselves as Americans and those who identify with their countries of origin.

If the minimum criteria model used in the logistic regression has a strong predictive ability, this it would indicate that those individuals who identify with the U.S. fit the criteria of being "American" better than those who identify with their countries of origin. Or, conversely stated, those who identify with their countries of origin, do not fit the criteria of being "American" as well as those who identify with the U.S. If, however, the logistic regression model is not a good predictor of identification with the U.S. or country of origin, then we would conclude that adherence to the characteristics of being American, as defined by the developed criteria, do not predict whether an individual will identify with the U.S. or their country of origin.

Additionally, these results will provide a groundwork of understanding which will help in conducting the focus groups interviews. For example, if the analysis were to find that political participation variables are not predictive, but language variables are predictive, then it might be suspected that the true underlying issue of national self-identification is not strictly political, but may be cultural in nature. This would alert the focus group facilitator to watch for or pursue indications of this possibility in the comments made during the interviews.

Focus Group Interviews

Although a careful examination of the NLIS data may take us a long way toward understanding the relationships between the criteria variables and the dependent variable of national self-identification, focus group interviews with Hispanic immigrants will provide further clarification of the results obtained through the empirical analysis. As observed above, the NLIS was not specifically designed to examine this issue of national self-identification. Further, the nature of telephone interviews like those conducted for the NLIS are generally such that the in-depth exploration of issues is not possible. Therefore, focus group interviews will be used to allow a group facilitator the opportunity to explore the feelings of the focus group participants with regard to this issue, and it will allow the participants the opportunity to more completely express their opinions.

Population to Be Studied

Because the purpose of the focus group interviews is to provide greater depth to the quantitative analysis done on the NLIS data, the population selected for the focus groups will mirror as much as possible the population of the NLIS. The population to be invited to the focus group interviews will be adult Hispanic immigrants, who have been legal residents in the U.S. for five or more years, living in areas of high, moderate, and low Hispanic concentration.

Approach/Methods Summary

The approach outlined above has the advantage of applying both quantitative and qualitative analytic techniques to the research question. The quantitative analysis of the NLIS data set will provide an examination of a large-sample-population and a statistical measure of the relationships between the criteria variables selected to represent being American and the dependent variable of national self-identification. The qualitative approach of the focus group interviews has as its strength the ability to provide a deeper understanding of the feelings and opinions of the focus group participants. Whereas the quantitative approach may allow us to see the relationships between, for example, civic participation and national self-identification, the qualitative approach will allow us to ask directly what they mean when they identify themselves as American or from their country of origin. It will also allow the exploration of what the respondents feel it means to be American.

The end result of using both quantitative and qualitative methods for addressing the research question will be a more complete picture of the differences in behaviors and attitudes of the respondents on both sides of this question; those who identify with their countries of origin and those who identify themselves as Americans.

CHAPTER 2

What is an American

Overview

America is a country built though immigration. With settlers from England, France, Spain, Germany, the Netherlands, Denmark, and other nations, arriving before the founding of the country, it is not surprising that Will Kymlicka in *Multicultural Citizenship* describes America as "the original immigrant country" (Kymlicka 1995, 61). Given the historical continuity of immigration to the U.S., it is understandable that Alejandro Portes and Rubén G. Rumbaut, in their work *Immigrant America*, would refer to America as a "permanently unfinished society," which has "become anew a nation of immigrants" (Portes and Rumbaut 1990, xvii). The impact of immigrants on the makeup of who is an American is noted by J. Harvie Wilkinson, III in *One Nation Indivisible*. He observes that "for the first time more Americans are descended from the forty-eight million who immigrated to the United States since 1790 than from those who lived in the United States before 1790" (Wilkinson 1997, 3).[10]

It is ironic that despite the historical importance and consistency of immigration, Americans have typically viewed the newest wave of immigrants with suspicion and concern. "We are a 'nation of immigrants' whose citizens have a long history of not supporting immigration" (Kolasky, 1997, 1). Espenshade and Hempstead also write that even though "the United States is frequently referred to as 'a nation of immigrants' there have been persistent attempts by former immigrants to keep out newcomers ever since the founding of the new colonies" (Espenshade and Hempstead 1996, 537). Lawrence Auster, writing in *Policy Review*, expresses similar sentiments when he refers to current immigration as a "Third-World invasion of this country" (Auster 1995, 88). He goes on to assert that this invasion is delegitimizing "American national identity and way of life" (ibid.). This attitude toward immigrants was evidenced in the results of a 1992 Harris study which asked *"Overall, over our history do you think immigration has been good or bad for this country?"* Thirty-four percent of those surveyed responded that they felt immigration had been bad for the country (Louis Harris 1992).[11] In March 2000, NBC News, Wall Street Journal survey had 51% of its respondents indicating they felt the United States was too open to immigrants.[12] Similarly, in response to a question on the General Social Survey in 2000, 43% of the respondents felt that immigration levels should be decreased.[13] In a Gallup poll conducted in September 2002, roughly one year after the 9/11 terrorist attacks, 54% of the respondents felt that immigration levels should be decreased.[14]

A concern regarding immigration among some seem to echo Auster's concern expressed above. In the 2000 General Social Survey, 73% of the respondents felt that more immigrants coming to this country would make, "it harder to keep the country united."[15]

Are immigrants leaving behind their loyalties to their native homelands and adopting America as their own? Are they becoming "Americans"? As noted in the introductory chapter, the NLIS data showed that legal Hispanic immigrants to the United States split almost evenly on the question of national self-identification: half saying they identify with America, and half identifying with their countries of origin. Results such as these in the NLIS and the continuing influx of immigrants lend support to those who have concerns that immigrants are changing America's national character, identity, and way of life.

But what does it mean to be "American"? As already mentioned above, America has been built by immigrants, and throughout its history each separate group of immigrants have added their distinct cultural flavor to the American culture. Across the centuries of our existence as a nation, the United States has adopted many customs, traits, holidays, foods, and verbiage of various immigrant groups. We celebrate St. Patrick's Day,

Cinco de Mayo, and Oktoberfest. We send our children to kindergarten (literally "children's garden" in German), say gesundheit (the German word for health) when someone sneezes, have our pie "a la mode" (French meaning after the fashion), or criticize an individual for trying to be macho (Spanish indicating masculine pride). We eat falafel, pizza, tacos, and sushi (although hopefully not all at the same meal), drink Irish coffee, and put salsa on bagels. Although it has not always happened immediately or smoothly, it nevertheless is true that adoptions or adaptations of many aspects of the varying cultures of immigrants have occurred, and America has come to claim them, in some form or another, as its own.

With so many influences from so many cultures, what is an American? By what criteria can someone be measured to determine how "American" they might be? If we could establish a set of minimum criteria for being "American," then we could return to the primary question of this research: Can a minimum set of criteria of what it means to be American predict whether an immigrant will identify with the U.S. or with their country of origin?

Historically, the criteria used to judge whether an individual was "American" appear to fall into two broad categories: 1) does the individual fit the ethnic, racial, or cultural criteria requisite to be an American, and 2) does the individual believe and practice the political principles, obligations, beliefs, and behaviors that make Americans American. Although historically, ethnic, racial, and cultural criteria have been used as a standard of being American, increasingly these criteria are being deemed inappropriate standards, as noted perhaps most importantly in Supreme Court decisions and through legislative action.

The objective of this chapter is twofold; first, by citing primary documents, academic discussion, and Supreme Court decisions, the chapter will briefly trace the historical use and decline in use of ethnic, racial, and cultural characteristics as criteria to determine who is an American. Second, the chapter will turn to the development of minimum criteria for defining who is an American based upon certain political principles, obligations, beliefs, and behaviors.

The search for some criteria for determining who might be an American should not be considered an onerous or invidious attack upon immigrants. By legally coming to and abiding in the United States, immigrants become part of the American social fabric and obtain the benefits and privileges which come with residence in the United States. The identification of a set of obligations, beliefs, and behaviors immigrants might be expected to live up to in return for belonging to the American social structure is in keeping with the political principle of citizenship having both rights and obligations (Janowitz 1980, 1). Although our populations of interest is all legal Hispanic immigrants and not only those immigrants who have obtained citizenship, it is not unreasonable to extend some of the obligations of citizenship to legal residents as well. While legal residents do not enjoy all of the benefits of citizenship, they do enjoy most of those benefits, and therefore it would seem reasonable that they would also incur some of the obligations.[16] But, in part because the population we are examining encompasses both citizens and non-citizen legal residents, it makes even more sense to seek to outline only a minimum threshold of what it means to be American, rather than an absolute or ideal standard.

Ethnicity, Race, and Culture as Criteria for Being American

Although America was built by immigrants, and at its founding as a nation the declaration was made that all men were created equal, Glazer contends "at every point in [American] history, the broadly inclusionary view can be contrasted with a narrow racist and chauvinist view" (Glazer 1996, 94). It was this narrower view of who can be American that was being expressed by Daniel Webster when he observed that America had been "established by the most earnest and resolute men of the most virile races the world has ever developed" (Brewer 1902, 15).

This firm belief that America was founded and populated by chosen people, people from the most "virile races," laid the groundwork for the use of what Smith in *Civic Ideals* describes as "ascriptive" criteria; race, ethnicity, gender and culture. As Smith notes:

> It is . . . unsurprising that many Americans have been
> attracted to ascriptive civic myths assuring them that,
> regardless of their personal achievements or economic

> status, their inborn characteristics make them part of a special community, the United States of America, which
>
> is thanks to some combination of nature, history, and God, distinctively and permanently worthy. (Smith 1997, 38)

The use of the ascriptive characteristics of ethnicity, race, and culture criteria in determining who qualified to be an American greatly limited the pool of who was eligible to be acknowledged as American. The argument was essentially:

- America is a special place for a chosen people.

- I, as an American, am one of the chosen, therefore,

- Other chosen people must be similar to me.

We will now briefly review the use of these ascriptive criteria throughout American history.

A Historical Review of Race and Ethnicity as Criteria for Determining Who Is American

The use of ethnicity and race as criteria for determining who could be considered an American has its foundation in attitudes and beliefs held long before the official formation of the United States as a nation. As noted by Horsman in *Race and Manifest Destiny*, as early as the seventeenth century, the concept of Americans as a "chosen people" permeated Puritan and then American thought (Horsman 1981, 3). It was not at all unusual for a people to consider themselves "chosen," but the American people could point to 'empirical' evidence of their being elect.

> God's intentions were first revealed in the survival and prosperity of the tiny colonies, elaborated by the miracle of a successful revolution against the might of Great Britain, and confirmed by a growth that amazed the world in the sixty years after that conflict. (Ibid.)

The use of ethnicity and race for defining who is an American is illustrated by the comments of Benjamin Franklin who observed the difference between resident, established "Americans", and new immigrant groups arriving on colonial shores. Franklin expressed his concerns that German immigrants in Pennsylvania were "too thick settled." Franklin thought Pennsylvania ran the risk of becoming a "Colony of Aliens" where the Germans would "Germanize" Americans instead of Americans 'Anglifying them . . .' (Carlson 1987, 26). Franklin, at this time, championed the notion of colonial and then later national homogeneity.

The assumption that Americans were homogeneous was expressed by John Jay in the *Federalist Papers* when he described Americans as:

> . . . descended from the same ancestors, speaking the
> same language, professing the same religion, attached
> to the same principles of government, very similar in
> their manners and customs. (*Federalist Paper* No. 2.
> Rossiter 1961, 38)

Fuchs notes that colonial Pennsylvania clearly took race into account in its settlement policies, welcoming only white European settlers on terms of equal rights. This use of race as a primary criteria for determining who could be an American was incorporated into the immigration laws of the new nation as a whole. Despite the need for labor, early immigration laws were nevertheless restrictive, showing preference toward white European immigrants. (Fuchs 1990, 8).

The belief of America being founded by a chosen race justified such restrictions and supported the contention that Americans were racially superior. The belief in the superiority of some races over others was clearly expressed in comments made by John Pinkerton in his work *A Dissertation on the Origin and Progress of the Scythians or Goths* (1787). He wrote:

> A Tartar, a Negro, an American [Indian] etc. etc. differ
> as much from a German, as a bull-dog, or lap-dog, or
> shepherd's cur, from a pointer . . . . The differences are
> radical; and such as no climate or chance could
> produce: and it may be expected that as science
> advances, able writers will give us a complete system
> of the many different races of men. (Horsman 1981,
> 31)

Jefferson expressed similar feelings regarding the superiority of Saxon heritage. In a letter to Edmund Pendleton written on August 13, 1776 Jefferson stated:

> Has not every restitution of the antient [sic] Saxon laws had happy effects? Is it not better now that we return at once into that happy system of our ancestors, the wisest and most perfect ever yet devised by the wit of man, as it stood before the 8th century? (Jefferson 1984, 752)

The Saxons had, per Jefferson, developed the best laws and were the people most capable of living in the system governed by those laws. This claim of racial superiority and of the superior heritage was, of course, attributed to divine mandate. Briggs describes early Americans as having the sentiment that "if ever God Almighty did concern himself about forming a government for mankind to live happily under, it was that which was established in England by our Saxon forefathers" (Briggs 1966, 6).

Despite the liberal sentiments put forward in the Declaration of Independence regarding the equality of men, it is clear that ethnicity, race, and culture were major factors in the conceptualization of who was an American in the early days of the nation. "There is no reason to suppose," writes Gordon, that the founding fathers "looked upon the fledgling country as an impartial melting pot for the merging of the various cultures of Europe, or as a new 'nation of nations,' or as anything but a society in which, with important political modification, Anglo-Saxon speech and institutional forma would be standard" (Gordon 1964, 90). America was to be, per Gordon's understanding of the founding fathers, a new Anglo-Saxon nation.

As the nation grew and expanded westward, Americans with increasing frequency began to populate areas already inhabited and claimed by other peoples; specifically Native Americans and Mexicans.[17] Armed conflicts arose as the United States conquered lands in its westward march. Since Anglo-Americans viewed themselves as a special people from a chosen race, it is easy to understand how they would view other peoples they encountered as inferior, particularly since they were of a different genotype. The belief that the peoples who inhabited the land

were inferior justified conquering the lands of western America and displacing the inhabitants. Anglo-Americans reasoned that if land was taken from the Native Americans or Mexicans, it was because the Native Americans or Mexicans were unfit to make proper use of the land. It was acknowledged that pain and suffering were being inflicted upon the existing inhabitants, but this was easily excused. "If the United States was to remain in the minds of its people a nation divinely ordained for great deeds," explains Horsman, "then the fault for the suffering inflicted in the rise to power and prosperity had to lie elsewhere" (Horsman 1981, 210). The fault lay in the inferior nature of the then current inhabitants. The suffering was their fault because they were not worthy to possess the land.
 With specific regard toward Mexicans, Horsman notes that the attitude was one that, "Mexicans had failed because they were a mixed, inferior race with considerable Indian and some black blood," (ibid.). The feelings of many in the United States in the early 1800's was that "the world would benefit if a superior race shaped the future of the Southwest," (ibid.).

 Horace Bushnell, speaking before the Society of Phi Beta Kappa Alpha of Connecticut at Yale College 1837, remarked that if the quality of the British people was changed into that of the Mexican "five years would make their noble island a seat of poverty and desolation" (Bushnell 1837, 9).[18] For Bushnell, God had reserved America for the special people of Saxon blood.

 The onset of the Mexican-American War (1846-1848) created a new context for discussing who could be "Americans." Specifically, the question at issue was whether Mexico should be conquered and incorporated into the United States. Although some supported the position of conquering Mexico and assimilating its population, to others the contemplation of incorporating Mexico was anathema because it would have meant the assimilation of a principally inferior "Indian" people. Senator John C. Calhoun firmly believed that the assimilation of the Mexican people would be a terrible error. He stated, "Ours, sir, is the Government of the white race," (U.S. Congress, Senate 1848, 98). Senator Jabez W. Huntington of Connecticut similarly argued against incorporating Mexico into the Union stating that the American constitution was not a constitution "for people of every color, and language, and habits" (U.S. Congress, Senate 1845, Appendix 397). As before, ethnicity and race are being used as key characteristics for describing who can be American.[19] Senator Huntington also added language and culture as critical to the definition of who could be an American.

The conclusion of the Mexican-American War did by no means lessen negative feelings toward non-Anglo immigrants. Politically, these nativist tendencies found voice through the American party, commonly known as the Know-Nothings. Before assuming the Presidency, Lincoln wrote:

> Our progress in degeneracy appears to me to be pretty rapid. As a nation, we began by declaring that '*all men are created equal.*' We now practically read it 'all men are created equal, except *negroes.*' When the Know-Nothings get control, it will read 'all men are created equal, except negroes, *and foreigners and Catholics*'. (Lincoln 1947, 214)

In the late 1800s, the demographics of the new immigrant waves underwent a significant change. The original or "old immigrants" to America had come from a relatively narrow geographic area of Europe. These immigrants were at least somewhat similar to the resident population in terms of race, political experience, economics, and social mores and practices. Hartman describes the old immigrants as having:

> . . . high standards of living, a low rate of illiteracy, a fairly active share in political self-government, and, with the exception of the German and Irish Roman Catholics, a uniform background of Protestant Christianity. . . . Although viewed generally with distrust and suspicion by many Americans upon their arrival, they adopted American ideals and habits easily and took their places as American settlers without too great a visible interference with the traditional American way of life. (Hartman 1967, 13-14)

The new immigrants of the mid- to late 1800s, however, were coming from regions of Europe which had not previously supplied population to America in appreciable numbers. These new immigrants came from:

> . . . the Russian Empire, Austria-Hungary, Italy, and the

Balkans-which were comparatively backward from a
political, social, and economic point of view when
compared with the regions of Europe which had sent
America its earlier type of immigrant. Standards of living
among these people were decidedly lower, illiteracy rates
ran high, experience with self government was practically
nil, and a subject 'race' status seemed to be the general
rule. Very few had the common background of Protestant
Christianity which had distinguished the great majority of
their predecessors and which was so characteristic of the
majority of native Americans at that time. (Ibid., 14-15)

If those immigrants who were similar in background to the
established American population were received with suspicion, it is of
little surprise that immigrants with fewer similarities would be received
with even greater antagonism (ibid., 17).

Waters in her book *Ethnic Options*, writing about two of these new
immigrant groups notes:

Italians . . . were one of the most despised groups. Old-
stock Americans called them wops, dagos, and guineas
and referred to them as the "Chinese of Europe" and
"just as bad as the Negroes." In the South some Italians
were forced to attend all-black schools, and in both the
North and the South they were victimized by brutality.
In 1875, the *New York Times* thought it "perhaps
hopeless to think of civilizing them, or keeping them in
order, except by the arm of the Law.'

The new immigrants were stereotyped as representatives of
some kind of lower species . . . . Greeks were physically attacked in
Omaha, Nebraska, and they were forced out of Mountain View,
Idaho. (Waters 1990, 2)

Cubberley, writing in 1909, described southern and eastern Europeans
as being "Illiterate, docile, lacking in self-reliance and initiative, and not
possessing the Anglo-Teutonic conceptions of law, order, and
government." He expressed concern that their arrival in America would
Adilute tremendously our national stock, and . . . corrupt our civic life.

(Cubberley 1909, 15-16). Cubberley is claiming as an Anglo-Teutonic characteristic the ability to deal with certain concepts of law, order, and government. The ability to deal with these concepts qualified those of Anglo-Teutonic heritage to be Americans. Conversely those of other races would have difficulty being Americans because racially they lacked this innate ability. Those new immigrants, being of a different racial/ethnic stock, would dilute these positive characteristics and corrupt American civic life. To Cubberley, race and ethnicity were considered essential in judging who qualified to be American.

Kenneth L. Roberts, in his article, *Why Europe Leaves Home*, very bluntly described the attitude of many Americans at the turn of the century toward the new immigrants. Many were concerned with keeping America pure:

> Races cannot be cross-bred without mongrelization, any more than a breed of dogs can be cross-bred without mongrelization. The American nation was founded and developed by the Nordic race, but if a few more million members of the Alpine, Mediterranean and Semitic races are poured among us, the results must inevitably be a hybrid race of people as worthless and futile as the good-for-nothing mongrels of Central America and southeastern Europe. (Roberts 1922, 22)

These feelings were not only directed to new immigrants from southern and eastern Europe, but also extended to the populations who recently had come under the American umbrella as a result of the Spanish-American War. Brewer, writing in 1902, reflected the concern of many Americas when he stated:

> Many of our citizens are to-day [sic] troubled by the fact that, as the outcome of the late war with Spain, we have taken distant islands with a large population of a character illy [sic] in accord with that of the Anglo-Saxon. We wonder what the outcome of this venture will be. (Brewer 1902, 54)

What had been avoided in the Mexican-American War, the subjugation of a large non-Anglo, non-European population, had come to pass in the Spanish-American War. These populations which came under the American umbrella were not considered, by many, qualified to be American specifically because they were not Anglo-Saxon.

This manner of thinking, equating being American with being Anglo-Saxon, has continued into the second half of the 20th century. In 1955, Will Herberg, writing in the *Protestant-Catholic-Jew*, observed:

> ... the American's image of himself is still the Anglo-American ideal it was at the beginning of our independent existence. The 'national type' as ideal has always been, and remains, pretty well fixed. (Herberg 1955, 33-34)

A 1988 California Poll asked the following question:

> *Because of immigration and other factors, the population of California is rapidly changing to include many more people of Hispanic and Asian background. Some people are worried that the changing makeup of California will make it hard to maintain American Traditions and the American way of life. Others say this is not a problem and that these groups quickly adapt. How about you? Would you say that you are very worried, somewhat worried or not at all worried about this?*

Over 50% of the respondents expressed some level of concern. Seventeen percent of respondents replied that they were very worried, with an additional 37% indicating that they were somewhat worried (California Poll 1988).

In 1996, a letter to the editor by Patrick J. McDonnell in the *Los Angeles Times* also expressed concern that immigrants were damaging the American identity.

> Today's near-record levels of immigration are deforming the nation's character. The inexorable influx, they warn could have dire long-term consequences: overpopulation, rampant bilingualism, reduced job opportunities for the native-born, and demographic shifts that could result in dangerous ethnic separatism. (Los Angeles Times August 11 1996, sec. A, 3)

The use of racial/ethnic criteria for determining who qualifies as an American still is used in some circles today. In his article in *Foreign Policy*, Huntington similarly expresses the concern that the influx of large numbers of Hispanic immigrants, particularly Mexicans, is an immediate and serious challenge to "America's traditional identity" (Huntington 2004). Glazer agrees that some consideration is still given to race as a qualifying criterion. He notes that given this criterion, one can be a citizen and yet not fully be an American:

> A strong accent, a distant culture, is no bar to citizenship, although it is clear that whatever we mean by the American nation, the new citizen may not yet be considered a full member of it by many of his fellow citizens, because of race or accent. (Glazer 1996, 87-88)[20]

As Carlson observes, the reality is that many "Americans rejected non-Caucasians, however Americanized, as a part of the national community" (Carlson 1987, 56). James Fulford, writing a wibzine response to an April 2001 National Review article by Ramesh Ponnuru states, " . . . it's *much* harder for visible minorities to forget their roots in foreign lands and assimilate than it is for whites" (Fulford 2004, emphasis in original).

> Americans have had a long tradition of using ethnicity and race for determining who is considered American. Brimelow perhaps summarizes these feelings best when he writes, "the American nation has always had a specific ethnic core. And that core has been white." (Brimelow 1995, 10)

A Brief Review of Culture as Criteria for Determining Who is American

Beyond ethnicity and race, cultural factors have also historically been used as criteria to determine who would be considered "American." Throughout American history there are those who have argued that immigrants must abandon their native cultures in order to become truly and fully American. Woodrow Wilson stated:

> America does not consist of groups. A man who thinks
> of himself as belonging to a particular national group in
> America has not yet become an American.
> (D'innocenzo 1992, 16)

The concern, as expressed by Horace Bridges in his book *On Becoming an American*, was that immigrants who maintained attachment to the cultures of their countries of origin would not become "American." Bridges, an immigrant himself, wrote, "All around us we find churches and schools and homes in which the Polish, the Greek, the Italian, or the German language is exclusively employed . . . ." The result, feared Bridges, would be that individuals raised under these conditions would have "dissociated" [sic] from their minds "the life and ideals of the [American] nation" (Bridges 1919, 123-124).

It would seem that the concern over an immigrant's loyalty to native culture emanates from equating cultural loyalty to national or political loyalty. This seems to be the issue Gordon is addressing when he states that if immigrants adopt American values and goals they will not impose "'alien' demands on the body politic" (Gordon 1964, 104). This concern was seen played out during the beginnings of the First World War. Prior to official U.S. entrance into the war, German-American cultural associations took a political stand and spoke out in favor of Germany in its conflict against France and England. In other words, principally cultural associations were taking a political position in favor of the country of origin of the members of the association. Bergquist, writes;

> For some German-American leaders and newspaper
> editors . . . especially those active in the National
> German-American Alliance, the support of German
> culture in America became identified with support of
> Germany's position in the European conflict.
> (Bergquist 1992, 66)

The question that needs to be answered then is how strong a connection is there between an immigrant's loyalty to his native culture and loyalty to his native country. If a strong connection does exist between the two, then abandonment of native culture would seem to be a legitimate condition to place upon immigrants in order for them to qualify as Americans. If however, there is only a limited connection or no connection between cultural and political loyalty, then abandonment of native culture would appear to be an unnecessary request to make of new immigrants.

Dahl is among the scholars who comments on the nexus between political culture and culture in general. Dahl expressed the opinion that political culture does not stand independent or unaffected by the broader culture of the people in which it exists (Dahl 1996, 3). With different groups having loyalties to various native cultures, a situation of hyper-egoism might result. Dahl describes hyper-egoism as a situation in which there would be a fragmentation of community interest and concern, with concern for either the individual or for a subgroup taking precedent to concern for the community as a whole. What would exist would be "a kind of polar antithesis to the politics of civic virtue" (ibid., 9-10). To maintain loyalty to a native culture rather than adopting the American culture may nourish these seeds of divisiveness. "Individual and group identities and loyalties" will exist, warns Dahl "at the expense of identification with a loyalty to the nation or the country" (ibid., 10).

Essentially this same sentiment was expressed from a slightly different perspective by Brewer who stated that loyalty to the United States must take precedence over all other associations. Brewer writes:

> Among the ideals filling the aspiring soul of every citizen of these United States should be the ideal nation. Neither himself nor his family, his friends, the community in which he lives, nor even the single State of which he is primarily a citizen should fill the measure of his thoughts and labors-but the great Republic, of which both himself and his family, friends, community and state are but parts, should ever rise like Mont Blanc among the Alps, the supreme object of devotion and toil. (Brewer 1902, 119)

An additional concern regarding immigrants maintaining ties to their native cultures was expressed by Philip Gleason. Beyond the possibility of political loyalty hiding beneath the surface of or masquerading as loyalty to culture, Gleason raises the concern that those who currently champion ethnic diversity (multiculturalism) implicitly deny the possibility for a "unitary *American* identity" based on agreement upon common principles (Gleason 1984). Schlesinger concurs, calling the desire to maintain ethnic/cultural identity the 'cult of ethnicity' which, he believes, is producing a divided nation of minorities rather than a unified America (Schlesinger 1992, 112). Petersen agrees, cautioning that one reason "some nation states have become weaker is that their ethnic components are stronger" (Petersen 1997, 277). Thus, maintenance of an immigrant culture may be anti-American, because it weakens America. Wilkinson expresses similar concerns when he writes:

> As our demographic picture becomes more diverse,
> as our shared social and cultural traditions become
> more varied, as our linguistic backgrounds become
> more diffuse, and as our separatist tendencies become
> more open and assertive, the concept of One Nation
> Indivisible is thrown into doubt. (Wilkinson 1997,
> 197)

Similar feelings have been expressed in more formal political settings as well. Senator Alan Simpson (R-WY), a participant on the Select Commission on Immigration and Refugee Policy, expressed his concerns in the supplementary comments to the final report. Senator Simpson wrote, "If linguistic and cultural separatism rises above a certain level, the unity and political stability of the nation will in time be seriously eroded" (U.S. Congress, Senate 1981, 6).[21]

Of our most recent immigrants, Brimelow, writing in 1995, states that they are ". . . from completely different, and arguably incompatible, cultural traditions"[22] (Brimelow 1995, 10). If maintenance of an immigrant's native culture is a threat to America, as these authors have postulated, the obvious solution, as seen by many, is that immigrants **must** integrate into the existing 'anglophone society' rather than forming separate enclaves representing their homeland cultures within the United States (Kymlicka 1995, 61-62). The historical American solution, Carlson observes, has been that immigrants must abandon their native manners of dress and grooming, and their native languages (Carlson 1987, 43). Specifically addressing Hispanic immigrants, Carlson goes on to state, " . . . Hispanics have a triple whammy, they are not Anglo, they are not Protestant, and they speak Spanish" (ibid., 56).

		WILL CALL AGAIN
		URGENT
		SPECIAL ATTENTION
...NTS TO SEE YOU		
RETURNED YOUR CALL		

Message _____

_____

_____

_____

_____

_____

_____

Signed _____

The Supreme Order
of the Star-Spangled
Banner
  └─ politicalparty
     └─ American Party

Legal Cases Supporting the Use of Ascriptive Criteria

One way of demonstrating the degree to which race, ethnicity, and culture were accepted as characteristics for determining who was an American is to examine Supreme Court decisions addressing this question. An examination of these decisions uncovers that through a large part of American history the social and political attitudes expressed in the above statements had legal sanction. As Smith writes, ". . . American law [has] long been shot through with forms of second-class citizenship, denying personal liberties and opportunities for political participation to most of the adult population on the basis of race, ethnicity, gender, and even religion" (Smith 1997, 2).

Beginning with the ratification of the Federal Constitution, legal context existed for the Court to use race as a characteristic for determining who fully qualifies as an American. One of the first issues addressed by the Constitution was of the organization of Congress, based on rules regarding enumeration to allocate representation to the differing states. Article 1 sec. 2 (3) distinguishes between, free persons, Indians not taxed, and "other" persons, meaning slaves. Only 3/5ths of slaves, essentially Blacks, were to be counted toward the enumeration. This Constitutional mandate, in effect declaring Blacks to be only 3/5 persons, provided a constitutionally based racial rationale for determining who could be fully American. After all, if Blacks did not merit consideration as full persons, they could hardly merit consideration as full Americans. The Supreme Court specifically commented on this concept in *Dred Scott v. Sandford*, 60 U.S. 393 (1857). Chief Justice Roger B. Taney, in delivering the majority opinion, posed the question as to whether Blacks were intended to be included as "people of the United States." He wrote:

> We think they are not, and that they are not included, and were not intended to be included, under the word 'citizens' in the Constitution, and can therefore claim none of the rights and privileges which that instrument provides for and secures to citizens of the United States. (Id. at 404)

Taney goes on to write that Blacks were "a subordinate and inferior class of beings, who had been subjugated by the dominant race, and

whether emancipated or not, yet remained subject to their authority . . . ."
Id. at 404. The language in this decision made it clear that the opinion of
the Court was that Blacks simply could not qualify to truly and fully be
Americans because they were racially an "inferior class of beings."

With the Civil War came the emancipation of the slaves and the
passage of the Thirteenth, Fourteenth, and Fifteenth Amendments. While
these Amendments were intended to erase the division between Whites
and Blacks, the legal opinion expressed in the *Dred Scott* decision — that
non-Whites were an inferior people not meriting full consideration as
Americans— continued to hold sway.[23] Additional opinions from the
Supreme Court strengthened the use of race as a criterion upon which full
standing in society could be granted or withheld.

In 1883, the cases which jointly became known as *The Civil Rights
Cases*, 109 U.S. 3 (1883) came before the Court. In 1875, Congress had
passed the Civil Rights Act prohibiting discrimination against any citizen
in the full enjoyment of public transportation, inn accommodations,
theaters, and other places of public amusement. The Supreme Court
ruled, however, that Congress had overstepped is authority, and therefore
the Civil Rights Act was unconstitutional. Although the decision was
based principally on legal questions regarding what constituted "state"
action, the decision effectively permitted the continued discrimination
against non-whites in public transportation, inn accommodations, theaters,
and other places of public amusement, thus maintaining the status of non-
whites as not fully American.[24]

In what almost seems like a reversal in their manner of thinking, in
1896 Congress would pass literacy tests as a means of limiting the number
of immigrants coming into the United States from undesirable countries.
First as a congressman and then as a senator, Henry Cabot Lodge (R-MA)
championed these tests believing they would be effective in weeding out
the inferior races which were "most alien to the great body of the people
of the United States." These included, "the Italian, Russian, Poles,
Hungarians, Greeks and Asiatics."   Conversely, English-speakers,
Germans, Scandinavians, and French would likely not be filtered out (U.S.
Congress, Senate 1896, 2817).

Measures had also been taken specifically against Chinese immigration. In 1882, Congress passed the Chinese Exclusion Act which was followed by even stricter legislation in 1884. As a result of these laws, Chinese individuals who had been resident in the U.S., but traveled abroad, could not return to the U.S. unless they had an identification certificate. In some cases even individuals who had been out of the country when the legislation was passed, and hence were physically unable to obtain the requisite identification certificate, were not allowed re-entry (Smith 1997, 366). Although overturning the decision in one such case, (*Chew Heong v. U.S.*, 112 U.S. 536 (1884)) Justice Stephen Field wrote in his dissenting opinion that the Chinese could not assimilate with the American people, yet were coming to the United States in "vast hordes." In 1888, Congress passed an even stricter law leading to what is known as the Chinese Exclusion Case, *Ping v. U.S.*, 130 U.S. 581 (1889). Chae Chan Ping had lived in California for twelve years. He left for China in 1887 with the then required re-entry certificate. He returned to California one week after the passage of the 1888 legislation, and was told his certificate was invalid and hence his re-entry illegal. The Supreme Court sustained the lower court decisions, and denied Ping entry into the U.S.

In 1891, the Supreme Court, with Justice Field now writing the majority opinion, upheld the dismissal of Chinese testimony merely on the basis of race (*Quock Ting v. U.S.*, 140 U.S. 417 (1891)). In 1892, Congress passed the Geary Act which, "presumed all Chinese" including U.S. citizens of Chinese descent, "to be deportable aliens unless they proved otherwise" (Smith 1997, 368). Some lower courts questioned the adverse assumptions of this legislation, but the Supreme Court in *Fong Yue Ting v. U.S.*, 149 U.S. 698 (1893) ruled the law to be constitutional. Although Justices Brewer, Fuller, and Field wrote a lengthy dissent, "no one made much of the fact that some U.S. citizens were now facing threatening requirements that others did not, simply because of their race" (Smith 1997, 369).

In 1896, the Supreme Court handed down its ruling in the landmark case of *Plessy v. Ferguson*, 163 U.S. 537 (1896). The Court interpreted the Fourteenth Amendment's provision for equal protection to be satisfied by the concept of separate but equal. This decision gave specific Supreme

Court sanction to the division of American society by race. The Court, in the majority opinion, specifically stated that legal distinction did not imply superiority and inferiority but merely provided for the "preservation of the public peace and good order." Although trying to walk a narrow line of allowing racial differentiation while not relegating a particular race to a lower and limited station in society, this is in fact what the Court did. In his dissenting opinion, Justice Harlan made two key observations. First, he noted, it was clear to all that the law Plessy was challenging had as its purpose "not so much to exclude white persons from railroad cars occupied by blacks, as to exclude colored people from coaches occupied by or assigned to white persons." And second, that "the white race deems itself to be the dominant race in this country." From Justice Harlan's point of view, separate but equal was merely a way of keeping non-whites from fully participating in the American mainstream; essentially from fully being American. Chase and Ducat, commenting on this case, observed ". . . it provided the legalistic smokescreen behind which an exploitive society operated for the next six decades" (Chase and Ducat 1979, 729). The effect of the decision was to allow legal sanction for limiting access of non-whites to certain aspects of the broader American society, including accommodations, transportation, restaurants, schools, etc. The impact was significant. As Smith writes in *Civic Ideals*:

> A few whites may have believed that they were creating a separate civic status for blacks that either was equal or on its way to being so. But most knew that they were making blacks second-class citizens at best, and many anticipated that under those conditions blacks would leave or, more probably, perish. (Smith 1997, 371-7)

Public transportation, restaurants, and schools were not the only aspects of society from which non-whites were excluded. Participation in political parties, and hence in the political process (the essential nature of which is discussed subsequently), was also restricted specifically by race.

In *Grovey v. Townsend*, 295 U.S. 45 (1935) Grovey, a black male, "citizen of the United States and of the state and county, and a member of and believer in the tenets of the Democratic Party," [295 U.S. 45, 46] residing in the state of Texas, petitioned the courts after having been denied an absentee ballot for a primary election solely on the basis of his race. This denial was in keeping with resolutions adopted at the Texas Democratic Party's state convention limiting party membership to whites only. Specifically, the resolution, adopted May 24, 1932 read:

> Be it resolved, that all white citizens of the State of Texas who are qualified to vote under the Constitution and laws of the state shall be eligible to membership in the Democratic party and as such entitled to participate in its deliberations. [295 U.S. 45, 47]

In *Grovey*, the court ruled that the action of the Texas Democratic Party Convention could not be deemed state action, and therefore did not fall under the purview of the 14th Amendment. This meant that the Texas Democratic Party could deny Grovey membership in the Democratic party and access to a ballot in the Texas primary elections solely based on his race. Given that the Democratic party was by far the majority party in Texas at that time, exclusion from the party essentially meant exclusion from any meaningful opportunity to influence the political process. Although other cases exist where different devices, such as poll taxes or literacy tests, were used to deny non-white populations from access to the polls, the Grovey case is noteworthy and cited here because the decision sustained the exclusion of individuals specifically and openly on the basis of race. Of this time period, Smith writes, "few judges denied that citizenship could be denied or limited on racial grounds" (Smith 1997, 365).

In *Hirabayashi v. United States*, 320 U.S. 81 (1943) and *Korematsu v. United States*, 323 U.S. 214 (1944) the Court sustained the use of curfews and military exclusion zones on the basis of race. In these cases, the curfews and military exclusion zones were applicable only to Japanese Americans, clearly differentiating the rights of individuals by ethnicity and race. In the dissenting opinion in Korematsu, Justice Jackson emphasized this distinction by race when he wrote that had the defendant been one of four individuals in that zone that evening, with the other three being "a German alien enemy, an Italian alien enemy, and a citizen of American-born ancestors, convicted of treason but out on parole— only Korematsu's presence would have violated the order . . . only in that he was born of different racial stock." [323 U.S. 214, 243]

In addition to these cases, other legal practices sustained the relegation of non-whites to marginal roles in American society. For example, non-whites were limited as to their opportunity to participate on juries; they were restricted as to where they could purchase property; laws were enacted and used to persecute their businesses; anti-miscegenation laws prohibited interracial marriages; and, of course, the right to vote among non-whites was limited through a variety of methods. Even from the few examples cited here it can been seen that ethnicity and race have been used as criteria to distinguish between who could fully participate in American society, and who could be legally kept at the margin of American society.

Ethnicity, Race, and Culture as Criteria for Being American: A Summary

What has been demonstrated in this discussion thus far is that for much of its history, America has used race, ethnicity, and culture as criteria for describing and determining who is an American. As Schlesinger observes, in his work *The Disuniting of America*:

> The [American] melting pot has had, unmistakably an inescapably, an Anglocentric flavor. For better or worse, the white Anglo-Saxon Protestant tradition was for two centuries--and in crucial respects still is-- the dominant influence on American culture and society. This tradition provided the standard to which other immigrant nationalities were expected to conform, the matrix into which they would be assimilated. (Schlesinger 1992, 28)

The use of these criteria have had legal sanction, beginning with a Constitutional decree that slaves were to be counted as 3/5 of a person, and have been supported for many years by decisions rendered by the Supreme Court. As Smith, in *Civic Ideals*, states:

> . . . when restrictions on voting rights, naturalization, and immigration are taken into account, it turns out that for over 80 percent of U.S. history, American laws declared most people in the world legally ineligible to become full U.S. citizens solely because of their race, original nationality, or gender. (Smith 1997, 15)

Expecting individuals to conform to the "white Anglo-Saxon Protestant tradition," as described by Schlesinger above, and enforcing those expectations by legal measures meant that to varying degrees, the ascriptive criteria of race, ethnicity, and culture, were the standard by which anyone trying to be an American was judged.

Problems in Using Ethnicity, Race, and Culture as Qualifying Criteria

The brief examination in the previous section has demonstrated how ethnicity, race, and culture have been used throughout much of American history as criteria to determine who qualifies to be considered fully an American. It is worth noting that the use of ethnicity, race, or culture as qualifiers is not unique to the United States. Germany, for example, has a very strong identity of a Germanic *people*. This sense of a German ethnic identity is still manifest in German immigration law which is based upon the principle of *jus sanguinis*, the right of blood. This *jus sanguinis* approach has been clearly demonstrated in how Germany has treated ethnic German refugees from Eastern Europe. These immigrants were "legally defined as Germans and immediately accorded all the rights of citizenship" (Brubaker 1993, 79). In stark contrast, children of Turkish "gastarbeiters" (guest workers), even though born in Germany, are not automatically granted German citizenship. German immigration laws are such that it is fully possible that neither the Turkish immigrant to Germany, nor his children or grandchildren born in Germany, might ever obtain German citizenship. Germany's "nationhood is an ethnocultural, not a political fact" (ibid., 81).

America, however, is not the same as Germany. Americans are not their own "people." Americans do not have a culture with a historic background such as the Germans. As Walzer states:

> It never happened that a group of people called Americans came together to form a political society called America. The people are Americans only by virtue of having come together. (Walzer 1990, 595)

Thus, a tension exists. For although, as was shown earlier in this chapter, "most white Americans throughout most of American history simply considered colored Americans inferior and unassimilable,"

(Schlesinger 1992, 58) people have come to reside in America not because it is an enclave of white Anglo-Saxon Protestantism, but rather because of the political, social, and economic freedoms America affords. And the acceptance of these immigrants, whether they are Anglo-Saxon or not, is sanctioned by the liberal political concepts of inclusion which have just as long a history in America as the belief in Anglo-Saxon superiority. The existence of simultaneous multiple traditions is a view supported by Smith, as he writes:

> This multiple traditions thesis holds that American political actors have always promoted civic ideologies that blend liberal, democratic, republican, and
>
> inegalitarian   ascriptive   elements   in   various combinations designed to be politically popular. (Smith 1997, 6)

The existence of simultaneous multiple traditions is evident when we read Franklin's concerns (cited above) about the increasing immigrant German population at roughly the same time that American political rhetoric is teaching that all men are created equal.

If we focus on the political philosophy that all men are created equal, then it is a natural progression to believe that all men should have an equal opportunity of becoming American, regardless of their racial, ethnic, or cultural background. Although, as has been pointed out above, this has not always been in the case in the past, it does appear to be the direction in which American society and Supreme Court legal decisions are moving. Many groups who were once shunned are now considered part of the American social, political, and cultural mainstream. Again, noting Franklin's concern for the increasing German immigrant population in his day, it is interesting to note that today Americans list Germany as an ancestral homeland on their census forms more often than any other single country. What at one point in time was a threatening immigrant group is now a standard "American" heritage. Similarly, in the mid to late 1800s, the large numbers of Irish-Catholic immigrants were viewed as a threat by the then established American population (Clark 1992, 77-102). Yet today one of our most fondly remembered presidents, John F. Kennedy, was of very publicly demonstrated Irish-Catholic ancestry. Across the centuries of our existence as a nation, Americans have in many respects behaved liberally in their adoption or adaptation of customs, traits, and verbiage of many different immigrant groups. As Americans we now find it acceptable to acknowledge or personally celebrate festival days which at one time were associated with disparaged ethnic immigrant populations. As previously noted, we celebrate St. Patrick's Day, Cinco de Mayo, and Oktoberfest. We use terms such as kindergarten (literally children's garden in German), gesundheit (the German word for health), a la mode (French meaning after the fashion), and macho (Spanish indicating masculine pride). We take some amount of pride in being experienced in eating a wide range of foods such as falafel, pizza, mu shu chicken, tacos, sushi, and Irish coffee. That salsa has become, in recent years, the number one condiment speaks volumes as to our acceptance of aspects of immigrant cultures. Throughout American history, the culture of immigrant groups has often been adopted or adapted, and America has often come to claim what were once immigrant customs as its own.

Thus, not only have once-shunned immigrant groups become part of the American mainstream, but increasingly, the use of ethnicity, race, or culture is being considered both socially and legally inappropriate as criteria by which to judge who qualifies as American.

This next section will now examine:

- the conceptual problems with using ethnicity, race, or culture as qualifying criteria for determining who is American, and

- the Supreme Court cases which have progressively declared the use of ethnicity and race unconstitutional as criteria for participation in varying aspects of American Society.

Conceptual Problems with Ethnicity or Race, as a Criterion

The use of ethnicity or race as a criterion for determining who is American suffers from four principal difficulties. These are:

- first, an ethnocentric approach violates the American liberal tradition of inclusion,

- second, Americans are not a people in any ethnic or racial sense,

- third, ethnicity or race is a poor discriminating criterion for detecting threats to the nation, and

- fourth, the use of race as a criterion specifically presents an unattainable standard for immigrants.

An Ethnocentric Approach Would Violate American Liberal Tradition of Inclusion.

Although, as has been demonstrated in the previous section, America has had a tradition of using race, ethnicity, and culture (an ethnocentric approach) as criteria for determining who can be considered an American, there are many scholars who argue that America has had a similarly strong tradition of liberal inclusion. Smith, for example, in his article *The "American Creed" and American Identity: The Limits of Liberal Citizenship in the United States*, although conceding that America has a long history of using ethnicity, race, and culture as criteria for determining "American-ness," also emphasizes that the United States has a strong tradition of liberal thought and rhetoric (Smith 1988, 226). These two traditions or lines of thought are in direct opposition. The American liberal tradition of inclusion, in declaring that all men are created equal, specifically disregards ethnicity, race, or culture as criteria for determining who is American. The existence of a liberal tradition does not in and of itself invalidate the ethnocentric approach. However, it does open the door for a reconsideration of using ethnocentric criteria for determining who is an American.

Many scholars and public figures have in fact compared the two approaches and selected the liberal approach over the ethnocentric approach. Kallen, for example, writing in the mid-1940s, effectively dismissed the ethnocentric approach in favor of the more liberal inclusive approach when he wrote that to impose "Anglo-Saxon conformity" upon immigrants to the United States violated the traditional American ideals of inclusion (Gordon 1964, 145). On the other hand, a liberal inclusive approach, which would result in cultural diversity, he described as being, "entirely in harmony with the traditional ideals of American political and social life." Kallen referred to the Declaration of Independence as an authorizing source to support the liberal inclusive approach. Kallen wrote:

> 'Equal,' in the intent of the Declaration . . . is an affirmation of the right to be different: of the parity of every human being and every association of human beings according to their kinds, in the rights of life, liberty, and the pursuit of happiness. (Ibid.)

Kallen is saying that it does not matter of what race or culture an individual may be, they still can qualify for the American benefits of life, liberty, and the pursuit of happiness.

Franklin D. Roosevelt would have concurred that race and ethnicity were not appropriate criteria for determining who was American. In 1943 he stated:

> Americanism is a matter of the mind and the heart; Americanism is not, and never was, a matter of race and ancestry. A good American is one who is loyal to this country and to our creed of liberty and democracy. (Schlesinger 1992, 37)

Almond and Verba express support for the liberal inclusive approach when they propose that it is acceptable for individuals to differ in religion and in other facets of their private lives as long as individuals act as good citizens of the American civic culture (Fuchs 1990, 5).

Jacobsohn, Jeffery, and Dunn, in their book *Diversity and Citizenship*, specifically write about the debate between multiculturalism and "cultural conception of nationhood," which emphasizes "the historic connections of the American people to a particular religious or ethnic tradition" (Jacobsohn, Jeffery, and Dunn 1996, xi). Regarding the ethnocentric or "cultural conception" approach, they conclude that

> . . . to the extent that this notion leads to depriving people of their full rights of citizenship solely on the basis of primordial attachments such as race, religion, or ethnicity, then such a definition is clearly incompatible

> with the logic of a nation defined by its dedication to
> certain "self-evident" principles of political morality.
> (Ibid.)

Although the arguments presented by the scholars above are not sufficient in and of themselves to discard the ethnocentric approach of determining who is American, they do point out the incompatibility of the ethnocentric approach with the long-standing American liberal tradition of believing that all men are created equal.

Americans are Not Truly a People

Americans are not a "people" in the same sense that the Germans, the French, the Chinese, the Japanese, or members of many other nations are distinct peoples. Walzer's statement, given above, is well worth repeating.

> It never happened that a group of people called
> Americans came together to form a political society
> called America. The people are Americans only by
> virtue of having come together. (Walzer 1990, 595)

Because the United States has been built by immigrants from countries and 'peoples' around the globe, they represent "every conceivable race, religion, [and] language group," and share, in Kymlicka's words "virtually nothing in common" (Kymlicka 1995, 61). It is specifically because they do not share a common history, culture, language, blood, or religion, yet have nevertheless coalesced into a nation, that Americans consider themselves exceptional. The concept of being American is based on common allegiance to a political system designed to accommodate wide differences (Harrington 1980, 678). If, as Harrington states, the true measure of being American is allegiance to a political system, then it is reasonable to accept Walzer's proposal that immigrants can retain "whatever identity they had before becoming Americans . . ." (Walzer 1990, 595).

Ethnicity or Race is a Poor Discriminating Criterion for Detecting Threats to the Nation

A concern which has often been raised is that non-Anglo immigrants pose a threat to our national security. This specifically was the issue in the

Hirabayashi and *Korematsu* cases cited above. Both Hirabayashi and Korematsu were convicted of violating regulations specifically aimed at curtailing the movements of individuals who were racially Japanese. But, as Justice Jackson emphasized in his dissenting opinion, these regulations would, in reality, have been ineffective protecting the military zones in question from a true German enemy, an Italian enemy, or a treasonous individual of American heritage. Justice Jackson specifically noted that Korematsu's presence in the exclusionary zone violated the order not because he was a threat, but only because of his "racial stock." [323 U.S. 214, 243] If there is a concern regarding the safety and integrity of the nation as a political entity and sovereign nation, the use of ethnicity, race, and culture does not provide accurate criteria by which to judge what individuals are truly a threat. There is no basis for assuming individuals of one ethnic group, or race, or culture are automatically more loyal to the United States or more of a threat to the nation's security. Hispanics for example earned 12 of 431 Medals of Honor in World War II, 9 of 131 Medals of Honor in the Korean War, and 13 of 239 Medals of Honor in the Vietnam war. Exact figures on the number of Hispanics serving in these conflicts are not available because the military, like the census bureau, did not at that time track Hispanics. Estimates place the number of Hispanics serving in Vietnam at 80,000 out of a total of 2.7 million. This would mean that although Hispanics represented only 3% of those deployed to Vietnam, they received over 5% of the Medals of Honor bestowed in that conflict.[25]

Race Is an Unattainable Standard for Immigrants

As stated at the beginning of this chapter, a principal objective of this chapter is ultimately to develop minimum criteria of what it means to be an American. For the criteria to be of any value, it must be at least theoretically achievable by the populations of interest, legal Hispanic immigrants. If a selected criterion is not achievable, it will be of no value in differentiating between those immigrants who identify as Americans and those who identify with their countries of origin, because neither group could meet that criterion. Ethnicity and race are unobtainable criteria because they would require the Hispanic immigrant population to become physically "white" to be considered American. This is obviously not an achievable goal. To select a criteria which could never be achieved which collectively became known as *Brown v. Board of Education*, 347 U.S. 483 (1954). Although the schools in Virginia and South Carolina were obviously and extremely unequal, the schools in Kansas were roughly comparable. Specifically because inequality was not at issue in the Kansas schools, the case turned on the question of whether segregation itself (the separate portion of separate but equal) caused inequality and was therefore unconstitutional. The Court ruled that it did, and through *Brown*, reversed and specifically rejected the 58 year old doctrine established in *Plessy*. Chief Justice Warren, writing the opinion of the Court, proposed that separating individuals, "solely because of their race generates a feeling of inferiority as to their status in the community" [347 U.S. 483, 494]. In this statement, Warren supports the concept, which has been developed in this work that, in part through legal decisions, non-whites had been relegated to a position of inferior status within the American community; they had been relegated to a position of being not quite fully American. Through *Brown*, the Court overturned *Plessy* and the doctrine of separate but equal, and thereby removed a major legal precedent which had been used to justify the use of race as a criterion for selecting who fully could participate as an American.

The Supreme Court's decision in *Brown* could be viewed as a beginning signal to significant changes in the legal atmosphere with regards to the broader inclusion of all populations into the broader American society. In 1957, Congress passed the first civil rights legislation since Reconstruction, PL 85-315, which made it a crime to prevent individuals from voting in federal elections. The Civil Rights Act of 1964, PL 88-352, barred discrimination in employment, public accommodations and federally funded programs, and created the Equal Employment Opportunity Commission. In 1965, Congress passed the Voting Rights Act, PL 89-110, which authorized federal examiners to register voters in areas which were determined to have been practicing discrimination.

In 1966 the Supreme Court handed down two key decisions, one related to the 1964 Civil Rights Act, and the other related to the 1965 Voting Rights Act. In *United States v. Guest*, 383 U.S. 745 (1966), six white males had been charged with violating the civil rights of Black individuals by, among other things, conspiring to "injure, oppress, threaten, and intimidate" Black citizens in the enjoyment and exercise of their 'right to travel freely to and from the State of Georgia" [383 U.S. 745, 757]. The charges had been dismissed by a lower court on the grounds that the indictment "did not involve rights which are attributes of national citizenship" [383 U.S. 745, 745]. The Supreme Court reversed and remanded the decision of the lower court. By doing so, the Court effectively affirmed a broad interpretation of the 1964 Civil Rights Act allowing its coverage to extend to the act of private individuals and not only state officials. The decision also gave a broad interpretation to the attributes of national citizenship, including in this case the right to unencumbered travel.

In *Katzenbach v. Morgan*, 384 U.S. 641 (1966), a challenge was brought to the court regarding the constitutionality of the Voting Rights Act of 1965 prohibition of New York elections laws requiring an ability to read and write English. The Court upheld the right of Congress to legislate a positive remedy to voting discrimination. Justice Brennan, writing for the majority, said, "The practical effect of 4 (e) is to prohibit New York from denying the right to vote to large segments of its Puerto Rican community. Congress has thus prohibited the State from denying to that community the right that is 'preservative of all rights'" [384 U.S. 641, 652].[28]

The Supreme Court's decision in *Loving v. Virginia*, 388 U.S. 1 (1967) to allow inter-racial marriage was another case which brought non-whites closer to a state of equality with whites in all aspects of society. In June of 1958, Mildred Jeter, a Black woman, and Richard Loving, a white man, both residents of Virginia, were married in the District of Columbia pursuant to its laws. After their marriage, they returned to Virginia to establish a home. In October of that year they were indicted by a grand jury and charged with violating Virginia's ban on interracial marriages. In January of 1959, they pleaded guilty to the charge and were sentenced to one year in jail. The trial judge suspended the sentence on the condition that the Lovings leave the state.

The Lovings left Virginia and took up residence in the District of Columbia, but in 1963 they filed a motion in the Virginia state trial court to vacate the judgment and set aside the sentence on the grounds that the statutes which they were convicted of violating, violated the Fourteenth

Amendment. The Lovings also brought a class action in the United States District Court. The case eventually found its way to the Supreme Court.

The importance of this case to the members of non-white populations seeking equal standing before the eyes of the law is attested to by a number of *amicus curiae* briefs filed with the court on behalf of various groups. *Amici curiae* briefs urging reversal of the convictions were filed by National Catholic Conference for Interracial Justice, the National Association for the Advancement of Colored People, and by the NAACP's Legal Defense & Educational Fund separately. Also, by special permission of the Court, William M. Marutani argued the cause for reversal as *amicus curiae*, representing the Japanese American Citizens League.

The Court overturned the conviction stating that it violated the Fourteenth Amendment even though it was argued that the law was being applied equally to blacks and whites. The Court reasoned that the purpose of the Fourteenth Amendment was to remove all sources of invidious racial discrimination in the States. Chief Justice Warren, delivering the opinion of the Court, made it clear that race was not an acceptable criterion upon which to base the rights of Americans. He wrote, "We have consistently denied the constitutionality of measures which restrict the rights of citizens on account of race" [388 U.S. 1, 11-12].

In 1968, Congress passed the Fair Housing Act, PL 90-284, which prohibited discrimination in the sale or rental of most housing. 1968 also saw the Supreme Court deliver a decision in *Jones v. Alfred H. Mayer Co.*, 392 U.S. 409, which upheld 42 U.S.C. 1982 which prohibited racial discrimination in the sale or rental of property. In this case, Joseph Lee Jones, a Black individual, brought suit against Alfred H. Mayer Co. alleging the respondent had refused to sell him a home on the sole basis that he was Black. Lower courts had dismissed the case concluding that 42 U.S.C. 1982 applied only to state action. The Supreme Court again gave a broader interpretation to the Law. Justice Stewart, delivering the opinion of the Court wrote:

> 1982 appears to prohibit all discrimination against
> Negroes in the sale or rental of property -
> discrimination by private owners as well as

discrimination by public authorities. Indeed, even the respondents seem to concede that, if 1982 "means what it says" - to use the words of the respondents' brief - then it must encompass every racially motivated refusal to sell or rent and cannot be confined to officially sanctioned segregation in housing. Stressing what they consider to be the revolutionary implications of so literal a reading of 1982, the respondents argue that Congress cannot possibly have intended any such result. Our examination of the relevant history, however, persuades us that Congress meant exactly what it said. [392 U.S. 409, 421-422]

Through this decision, the Court ruled against another manner in which non-white populations had been kept out of the mainstream of American society.

Summary of Legal Cases

Previously in this chapter, Supreme Court cases were cited which supported the use of race and ethnicity as criteria for determining who could fully participate in U.S. society. In this section we have reviewed Supreme Court cases which have ruled in the opposite direction, namely that race and ethnicity are not acceptable criteria for making this determination. Although the cases discussed in these two sections are certainly not an exhaustive list of all cases decided by the Court in this area, as is illustrated in table 1, these cases do demonstrate the shift in the thinking of the Court on the use of race and ethnicity as criteria for determining who is fully a member of the American community.

Table 1. Summary of Law Cases

Year	Use of Ascriptive Criteria Acceptable	Use of Ascriptive Criteria Unacceptable
1857	*Dred Scott v. Sandford* Blacks described as an inferior class of beings	
1880		*Strauder v. West Virginia* Blacks cannot be excluded as jurors
1883	*The Civil Rights Cases* Congress overstepped its bounds. Ruling permitted continued discrimination in public transportation, inn accommodations, theaters, and other places of public amusement	
1886		*Yick Wo v. Hopkins* Discriminatory application of a local law ruled a violation of Equal Rights Clause
1893	*Fong Yue Ting v. U.S.* Sustained Geary Act deeming all Chinese to be deportable unless they could prove otherwise	
1896	*Plessy v. Ferguson* Established separate but equal doctrine	
1935	*Grovey v. Townsend* Political parties can limit membership by race	
1944		*Smith v. Allwright* Political parties cannot limit membership by race

Table 1. Summary of Law Cases, cont.

Year	Use of Ascriptive Criteria Acceptable	Use of Ascriptive Criteria Unacceptable
1943	*Hirabayashi v. U.S.* Race can be used in creating and enforcing military exclusion zones	
1944	*Korematsu v. U.S.* Race can be used in creating and enforcing military exclusion zones	
1948		*Shelley v. Kraemer* Restrictive covenants prohibiting sale to Blacks or Asians violates 14th Amendment
1954		*Brown v. Board of Education* Separate but equal doctrine overturned
1966		*United States v. Guest* Affirmed broad interpretation of 1964 Civil Rights Act
1966		*Katzenbach v. Morgan* Affirmed proactive nature of 1965 Voting Rights Act
1967		*Loving v. Virginia* Antimiscegenation statute ruled to violate 14th Amendment
1968		*Jones v. Alfred H. Mayer Co.* Applied statute outlawing discrimination in sale or rental of property to private as well as state action.

Although cases regarding the use of racial and ethnic criteria would continue to be brought before various courts, it is clear with the statement of Chief Justice Warren above, that race as a determining criterion for who qualified for full acknowledgment and benefits as an American was no longer acceptable and deemed unconstitutional.   Wilkinson summarizes the current situation well when he writes:

> We stand before the law as equals. Its commands speak to the citizen, not to his race. The Anglo American and the Hispanic American pay the same taxes and obey the same speed limits as the Asian American and the African American. (Wilkinson 1997, 83)

Loyalty to Native Culture: The Remaining Question

Thus far we have shown how the use of the ascriptive criteria of ethnicity and race are logically unsustainable and have in the last half of the 20th century been declared illegal for determining who can fully participate in American society. Even after removing the social and legal justifications for use of ethnicity and race as qualifying criteria, however, one additional question remains. If an immigrant maintains a preference to the culture of his country of origin, should this disqualify him from being considered an American? Is cultural allegiance an appropriate criterion for determining who is an American?

As cited above, Wilson stated:

> America does not consist of groups. A man who thinks of himself as belonging to a particular national group in America has not yet become an American. (D'innocenzo 1992, 16)

While there are those who are concerned with immigrants maintaining cultural loyalties, often because they equate cultural loyalty to political loyalty as noted by Bergquist above, there are others who see these concerns as overblown. Harrington, for example, believes that at some point the concerns regarding an immigrant group maintaining a native culture is "nothing more than the . . . force of racial and ethnic prejudice" (Harrington 1980, 680). Harrington is saying that what may drive the concern over, for example, Mexican immigrants celebrating Cinco de Mayo is not that it might be an expression of latent political loyalty to their native country, but rather simple prejudice against non-white Mexicans. Harrington is raising the possibility that it isn't culture at all or its possible connection to political loyalty, but rather simply prejudice against the immigrant population which is at the root of expressed concerns over attachment to native culture.

Although Harrington raises a valid concern that some of the objections to maintaining native cultural attachments may simply be latent prejudice, this does not completely eliminate the concerns over immigrants maintaining loyalty to their native cultures. However, to validate the concern that cultural loyalty belies political loyalty, to move this concern beyond the realm of mere xenophobia, it would need to be demonstrated that there is a connection between loyalty to native culture and political loyalty to native country. The additional step would also be required of showing that this political loyalty to native country is at conflict with loyalty toward the United States. While it may be conceded that, as Harrington states, "Loyalty to the United States requires that at some point ethnic group demands for the homeland must be subordinated to the larger interests of [this] country," meaning the U.S., this does not, as Harrington also points out, absolutely preclude some continued attention to the needs of an immigrant's homeland (ibid., 683). Further, exactly at what point loyalty to the United States limits or precludes immigrants maintaining attachments to the native cultures, or the promotion of political causes in their homelands has been, since World War I, a very difficult point to determine and a subject of considerable debate (ibid., 678). Harrington correctly points out that requirements of loyalty in this regard have never been clearly defined by law, but more often have been drawn by public opinion. If a line has been drawn at all, writes Harrington, "[it] has been drawn largely by popular reaction, incident by incident, to various ways ethnic groups have been involved in affairs of their homelands" (ibid., 679-80).

In fact, at times the appeals of immigrants for causes in their homelands have, as Harrington writes, "aroused positive public enthusiasm . . ." (ibid.). At times then, the connections immigrants had to their native countries, and the expressions of concern for political affairs in those countries became a concern for the broader U.S. population.

Certainly the concern remains that the hyper-egoism Dahl warns of, the concern for the narrow interests of a particular group (see page 31), might result if different groups become focused only with affairs that affect them in particular.[29] Other scholars consider the attempt to influence American politics for the benefit of a societal sub-group one of the more American things immigrants could do. Huntington states, "American history is the history of the efforts of groups to promote their interests by realizing American ideals" (Huntington 1981, 11-12).

The connection between maintenance of an immigrant's culture and the likelihood of a dangerous level of retained political allegiance to an immigrant's country is at best tenuous, and is further weakened by the fact that in some cases the culture which an immigrant maintains does not or cannot equate to loyalty to a native country. In some cases the attachment to a supposed 'native' culture is actually an attachment to a social construct which does not even exist outside of the United States. Over time, some established immigrant communities in the United States developed their own culture similar to but different from the culture in their native lands.

Early German immigrants illustrate this point well. Franklin's previously cited comments regarding German immigrants, seems to imply that the German immigrants were a homogenous group coming from a common background in the Old Country. In actuality, German immigrants at that time were both Protestant and Catholic, spoke varying regional dialects, and had different regional loyalties. There would be, in fact, no unified German nation for another 100 years. It was the juxtaposition of their native cultures to the American culture that effectively reconfigured their ancestral identity and constructed a common German identity here in America.

Hispanic immigrants today are also not a homogeneous group, but rather are very heterogeneous. They come from different nations with widely varying national cultures, as well as widely varying cultures within their countries of origin. As with the early German immigrants, what often unites Hispanic immigrants in the United States is a common language, and the juxtaposition of their native cultures to the American culture.

Cuban Americans pose a slightly different example. Although the Cuban American population in the United States is very cohesive, and they all have loyalty to a common homeland, the homeland to which they have loyalty, is to a non-Castro Cuba; a Cuba which exists only in exile in the United States.

If the loyalties to native culture expressed by some immigrants are in fact loyalties to a American construction of their native culture, then it is less likely that this loyalty to culture will cause loyalty to a political entity other than the U.S. It is perhaps with this realization that Franklin eventually overcame his earlier concerns about immigrants, and:

> Thought it sufficient proof of fealty to republican ideals and principles of government [that] individuals had left the countries of their birth and had chosen to live in the new nation. (Kettner 1978, 227)

If they want to be in the United States, Franklin is saying, if they have made the effort to come here and have settled here, this is evidence of their desires to be American.

Jacobsohn similarly believes immigrants have come to America with aspirations of "political unity, not cultural unity." The grand purpose had among the waves of immigrants who have come to America is to "become American citizens, not to abandon their cultural, religious, and ethnic backgrounds" (Jacobsohn, Jeffrey, and Dunn 1996, xv).

In the recent report entitled "Legal Immigration: Setting Priorities" from the Congressional Bi-partisan Commission on Immigration Reform, the commission wrote "that religious and ethnic diversity are compatible with national civic unity in a democratic and free society." Very specifically they noted that, "Religious and cultural diversity does not pose a threat to the national interest as long as public policies ensure civic unity" (U.S. Commission on Immigration Reform 1995, xxxi).

The connection, then, between an immigrant's loyalty to his native culture and disloyalty to the United States, is at best very weak. Although the level of an immigrant's political allegiance to native homeland might be worth questioning if perhaps there was armed conflict with an immigrant's country of origin, there is insufficient connection between attachment to native culture and political allegiance to native homeland to justify making loyalty to native culture a reason for excluding someone from being considered an American.[30] As observed by Gans, the cultural identification of immigrants with their countries of origin is more likely than not symbolic in nature, rather than political (Gans 1979) .

Even dismissing the threat of diminished political loyalty toward the U.S. resulting from a recent immigrant's continued attachment to their native cultures, some are distressed at the infusion of foreign culture brought by waves of immigrants, and they fear its effects upon American culture (as if American culture were homogenous). For example, as noted above, McDonnell fears that the new immigrants are deforming America. This concern is not shared by all, however. Both Clyde Kluckhohn in 1958 and Seymour Martin Lipset in 1963 concluded that "there is more continuity than change with respect to the main elements in the national value system" (Huntington 1981, 21). Further, America does not consist of a homogeneous culture, nor are there single cultures within most countries on the globe. Thompson, Ellis, and Wildavsky observe in their book *Cultural Theory* that "competing ways of life exist within" any single nation (Thompson et.al. 1990, 215). Gordon, in explaining the existence of multiple cultures within one national society, explains that we exist within several concentric circles of social interaction. Our ethnic or cultural identity exists within one circle, but this circle does not necessarily interfere with our sharing "political participation, occupational relationships, common civic enterprise, perhaps even an occasional warm friendship" (Gordon 1964, 29) with those outside our circle living in circles of their own. Everyone exists within some type of circle. Even the Anglo-American, the archetypal American, from whom most of the protest regarding ethnic/cultural identity has come, inhabit such groups. As Gordon notes, however "the white Protestant American, is rarely conscious of the fact that he inhabits a group at all. *He* inhabits America. The *others* live in groups. One is reminded of the wryly perceptive comment that the fish never discovers water' (ibid., 5).

Benefits from Maintaining Ethnic/Cultural Links

In contradistinction to considering the maintenance of cultural links by recent immigrants a threat, several scholars contend cultural maintenance may actually provide benefits not only to the immigrants, but to the nation as well. One benefit cited by Michael Novak in regard to the immigrants from eastern and southern Europe was that by remaining as groups, .

immigrants maintain a vital sense of family and community which in his opinion are worth nurturing (Novak 1973).

Ungar in his work *Fresh Blood: The New American Immigrants*, concurs with Novak. He not only dismisses the use of ethnicity, race, and culture as reasons to be suspicious of new immigrants, but he also believes the new immigrants are of benefit to America. Ungar writes:

> In an era of crass materialism and widespread, growing cynicism, immigrants help renew, enrich, and rediscover the values of America [the immigrants] remind us of ideals to often forgotten, except in empty political dialogue, in America today: the value of family, respect and care for our elders, kindness and compassion for a larger community of interest. (Ungar 1995, 368)

Ungar goes on to state that the only reason for opposing immigration is racism of one form or another (ibid.).

The sense of community mentioned by Novak and Ungar brings about another benefit which at first glance appears to be counterintuitive, that being that loyalty to native culture may ultimately assist the immigrant to assimilate into American society. "The self-contained communal life of the immigrant colonies," suggests Gordon, served "as a kind of decompression chamber in which the newcomers could, at their own pace, make a reasonable adjustment to the new forces of a society vastly different from that which they had known in the Old World" (Gordon 1964, 106). That such enclaves should develop was only natural according to Hartman. Challenged by a new language, surroundings, and missing his native environment, an immigrant found in an ethnic or cultural enclave, security, safety, and advice from those who had arrived before (Hartman 1967, 16).

Fuchs agrees noting:

> Immigrants of different backgrounds found it was to their advantage to establish a new identity as ethnic-Americans . . . . The process of reconfiguring their ancestral identity was one other groups would go through, too, including various Filipino and Chinese

century.   Personality traits, social characteristics, geographic and environmental features, behavioral patterns, and historical experiences have all been invoked by one analyst or another. (Ibid., 13)

To develop the absolute definition of the American creed or the American national identity is beyond the scope of this examination. The objective here, as expressed at the beginning of this chapter, is to develop criteria which make up a minimum threshold of what it means to be an American. Having dismissed ascriptive criteria for determining who is American, but assuming, as Huntington, Bridges, and others suggest, that there exist a set of core duties, values, beliefs, or behaviors which constitute being American, the task now is to discover and enumerate what those core duties, values, beliefs, and behaviors are.

In relationship to immigrants, the most common mentioned duties, values, beliefs, or behaviors mentioned in academic and political discussions can be subdivided into two major categories. These are:

1. belief in the American system of government, and

2. living a moral, civic life, which consists of three dimensions:

    •   participating in voluntary organizations for the good of the community,

    •   participating in the political/electoral process, and

    •   learning English sufficient to be able to participate in the political process.

I will now discuss each one of these categories.

Belief in the American System of Government

As noted above, for most nations, national identity is based upon "a long process of historical evolution involving common ancestors, common experiences, common ethnic background, common language, common culture, and usually common religion" (ibid., 23). This is not the case in the United States. As observed by Walzer, cited previously, there never was a group of people called Americans who came together and formed a society called America (Walzer 1990, 595). Americans are Americans by virtue of believing in certain political principles and by coming together in political union based upon those principles.

Petersen advances this line of thought in his work *Ethnicity Counts*. Petersen proposes that because Americans lack "a natural unity based on biology or a common history" they sought their tradition elsewhere. Quoting historian George Bancroft (1800-1891), Peterson writes that Americans, "seized as their particular inheritance the tradition of liberty" (Petersen 1997, 52). Americans have come to rely upon political principles, and, most importantly, on their tradition of liberty as unifying factors to bind them together as a "people" and a nation. Huntington comments on the unique importance of political principles in defining who is an American when he observes that in other countries one can abrogate the constitution without abrogating the nation. This is certainly the case with Germany where German peoplehood exists independent of the existence of a particular form of German government. Americans, however, are Americans because of the existence of the Constitution, the political principles there embodied, and the resulting nation it created (Huntington 1981, 30).

This political foundation to American "peoplehood" has given Americans, from very early in their history, a peculiar political manner of being. Carlson notes this when he writes that Americans have "a Civic Religion that all those who wish to be American must conform to" (Carlson 1987, 56). Carlson is echoing the observations of Francis Grund written in his book *The Americans*. In 1837 Grund wrote that the political doctrines of America were "the religion and the confession of the people. . . ." (Grund 1837, 149-50). Grund emphasized this point by writing:

> It was the genius of liberty which gave America a national elevation . . . It is the bond of union, the confession, the religion, the life of Americans; it is that which distinguished them above all other nations in the world. (Ibid., 107)

By using terms such as, "the religion and the confession of the people," Grund is saying that the cultural fabric which holds other peoples together, is among Americans replaced by the belief and practice of certain political doctrines; specifically those political doctrines surrounding liberty.

Francis Wright also noted the importance of the belief and practice of certain political doctrines in defining who was an American. "They are Americans," Wright declared "who, having complied with the Constitutional regulations of the United States . . . wed the principles of America's Declaration to their hearts and render the duties of American citizens practically in their lives" (Fuchs 1990, 21). Fuchs, interpreting Tocqueville, observes that Tocqueville had discovered that, "what distinguished the American national spirit, character, and identity was not sectarian religion or ancestry but a culture of politics" (ibid.).

Abraham Lincoln also viewed the belief in American political principles not only as something that immigrants needed to acquire, but also as something that would transform the immigrants themselves. Observing in 1860 that the largest group of immigrants at the time were German and could not identify with the Revolutionary War, Lincoln expressed the opinion that they could nevertheless identify personally with America because:

> . . . when they look through that old Declaration of Independence, they find that those old men say that 'we hold these truths to be self evident, that all men are created equal,' and then they feel . . . that they have a right to claim it as though they were blood of the blood and flesh of the flesh of the men who wrote the Declaration of Independence." (Eastland 1979, 53)

The belief in those principles expressed in the Declaration of Independence, Lincoln is saying, would make Americans of immigrants just as much as if in their veins ran full with the inherited blood of the founding fathers.

This line of thought, that allegiance to political principles is what changes immigrants into Americans, was reiterated in the early 1900s in President Woodrow Wilson's comments to a group of newly naturalized citizens. He followed this theme of allegiance to political principles being critical to making immigrants American when he commented on the naturalization oath itself. He observed that the new immigrants had sworn allegiance to "a great ideal, to a great body of principles . . ." (Harrington 1980, 678).

The uniqueness of having the system of government being a unifying factor and a primary component of national identity is discussed in the writings of Almond and Verba. As they report in their book *The Civic Culture*, when respondents were asked what they were most proud of with respect to their countries, approximately 85% of American mentioned some aspect of their political tradition, the American political tradition. When the same question was asked of citizens of other countries, the results were markedly different. Only 46% of British, 30% of Mexican, 7% of German, or 3 % of Italian respondents made mention of their political traditions. (Almond and Verba 1965, 64-65).[31]

To be an American, then, means to believe in the American system or culture of governance. But can we even further define what this means?

Huntington believes the most often cited values of American political system to be "support for liberty, democracy, majority rule, minority rights, freedom of speech and religion," and equality (Huntington 1981, 18).[32]

Fuchs writes that from early in American history:

> . . . spokesmen for the new American nation explained that the U.S. was created by God as an *asylum* in which *liberty, opportunity,* and *reward for achievement* [emphasis in original] would prosper. (Fuchs 1990, 2)

Liberty, according to Fuchs, was not merely believed in as a national political principle, but as a governing principle which was of divine mandate. He continues by observing that this belief in a divine nature and purpose for the United States became the foundation of American political culture, and encouraged the uniting of "Americans from different religious and national backgrounds," into one nation (ibid.).

Understanding and believing in liberty as a political concept before one could become an American is a qualification that has been supported since the earliest days of this nation. This support is evidenced in comments from members of Congress early in the existence of the Union. Representative Theodore Sedgewick of Massachusetts (1796-1799) expressed the concern that some immigrants having been subjects of "despotic, monarchical, and aristocratical" governments would be allowed "as soon as they set foot on American ground . . . to participate in administering the sovereignty of our country." (U.S. Congress, House 1794, 1006). He did not feel they would be prepared for such a duty. Representative Thomas Hartley of Pennsylvania (1789-1800) similarly expressed his concern about granting to immigrants the rights and responsibilities of citizenship before sufficient time had passed for them to have, "an opportunity of esteeming the government from knowing its intrinsic value" (U.S. Congress, House 1790, 1109). By government he specifically meant the type of government had in the United States: American Democracy. Representative Michael Stone of Maryland (1789-1791), also wanted a longer waiting period before immigrants could apply for naturalization; one long enough to guarantee that immigrants would "have acquired a taste for this kind of government" (ibid., 1118). A belief in or taste for liberty and the American form of government was requisite for immigrants to acquire, in the minds of these early Congressmen, before qualifying to be American.

It is clear then, that from its inception, the Americans have viewed themselves as believing in a unique set of political principles most often including belief in and support of liberty, democracy, majority rule, minority rights, and freedom of speech and religion. As expressed by the scholars and political figures cited above, belief in these political principles is one of the principal characteristics of being an American.

Living a Moral, Civic Life

Beyond the belief in American political principles, several authors propose that living a moral civic life is an important dimension of what it means to be an American. Brewer for example, in his book *American* .

Citizenship, argued that high moral standards and good character were a national duty. While never fully defining good character, Brewer does include the ideals of truth, justice, honesty, and purity (Brewer 1902, 51).[33] Brewer goes on to write that Americans must "lift their eyes above the narrow horizon of their own convenience . . . and see that in the performance of those duties they are doing their part in helping the nation to its highest usefulness . . ." (ibid., 70). The duty of a good American, Brewer is saying, is to look beyond merely their own needs, and look to the needs of the nation as a whole. The end result of doing this is a public good: improvement to the general welfare of the nation.

Dahl believes that helping one another for the good of the nation should be the motive for involvement in political life. The ideal society, believes Dahl, would be one in which "citizens engage in political life with the primary goal of achieving the public good, or the general welfare, or the good of all, or the public interest" (Dahl 1996, 1). This is what Dahl refers to as "civic virtue." Although this is what Dahl views as the ideal situation, he does not really believe it possible to achieve this state in a large diverse democracy. Specifically he notes that a society ruled by civic virtue would require,

> a body of people so homogeneous in their conceptions of
> their interests that sharply conflicting and partial views
> of the public good would not arise, or if they did would
>
> be quickly and overwhelmingly dismissed by a
> preponderant majority of citizens. (Ibid. 4)

Where such homogeneity does not exist, Dahl's concern, as noted previously, is that society will be based upon hyper-egoism with an individual's concern for himself, or for the subgroup of society to which he belongs, taking precedence over cooperation and concern for society as a whole. Dahl gives as examples the societies as proposed by Thrasymachus in *Plato's Republic*, by Machiavelli in *The Prince*, or by Hobbes in *The Leviathan*. Dahl's solution is a society based upon what he refers to as "robust civility." Dahl's robust civility is a compromise between civic virtue and hyper-egoism. "It needs less nobility[34] than civic virtue requires, [yet] it provides more civility, decency, sympathy, and generosity of spirit than can be found in the politics of hyper-egoism" observes Dahl (ibid. 11). Robust civility would allow for the expression of individual sentiments and concerns, within the existence of a heterogeneous polity, but a polity in which all the citizenry jointly search for that which is of value to the larger community or the nation as a whole (ibid. 13).

That an obligation exists for members of a society to seek to do that which is of value to the larger society was a theme also addressed by T.H. Marshall, in his book *Class, Citizenship and Social Development*. He specifically enumerates "promoting the welfare of the community" as a obligation critical to good citizenship (Marshall 1973, 93). Although some might find the term "obligation" harsh or coercive, Janoski and other scholars strongly believe obligations are absolutely needed. In his book *Citizenship and Civil Society*, Janoski marvels in fact at the, "chronic avoidance of obligations." Janoski believes that, "rights require obligations for their fulfillment, since no right may exist without an obligation to help make the right exist . . ." (Janoski 2000, 53).

The broad statement that Americans should seek to do that which is of value to the larger community seems to create great latitude, if not a virtual total lack of definition, as to what obligations this might place on an immigrant.

However, particularly when the discussion regarding new immigrants are examined, many of the possible obligations appear to fall into the following three categories;

1. participation in voluntary associations,

2. participation in the political/electoral process, and

3. learning English sufficient to be able to participate in the political process.

We shall now turn our attention to each of these categories.

Participation in Voluntary Associations

As noted above, Marshall proposed that promoting the welfare of the community was an obligation of good citizenship. However, even by Marshall's own admission, the goal of promoting the welfare of the community was vague and ill-defined. Janowitz sought to more specifically define this obligation by proposing that one manner in which the welfare of the community can be promoted is by individuals participating in voluntary associations, especially those which are community based (Janowitz 1980, 16-17). James Sellers, in his book *Public Ethics: American Morals and Manners*, similarly observes that the spirit of citizenship in a republic requires citizens to take action, "especially that kind of action that expresses willingness: initiative" (Sellers 1970, 73). The citizens, or community residents, must of their own accord be involved in the community.

Hardy-Fanta, among others, makes it clear that this type of action need not be limited to those areas which are typically classified as political. "What is political?" she inquires, then responds by observing that in the case of Latina women, often their political actions take place as a mobilizing force of community service within the Latino community (Hardy-Fanta 1993, 15). Tilly and Gurin use the term protopolitics to describe these "political" activities which are "unmediated by organization" but rather are mediated by relationships (Tilly and Gurin 1990, 7). Redefining political participation to include community service and community action is a critical clarification of the definition. Without this clarification in the definition of what is political, certain populations, such as Latina women, would be, according to Hardy-Fanta, politically invisible, appearing not to be participants in the political process. In reality, their involvement in building the community, in building America, is significant.

Tocqueville similarly observed the importance of these non-political associations in building America when he wrote:

> The Americans make associations to give entertainments, to found seminaries, to build inns, to construct churches, to diffuse books, to send missionaries to the antipodes; they found in this manner hospitals, prisons, and schools. If it be proposed to

inculcate some truth, or to foster some feeling by the encouragement of a great example, they form a society. Wherever, at the head of some new undertaking, you see the government in France, or a man of rank in England, in the United States you will be sure to find an association. (Tocqueville 1984, 198)

Judith N. Shklar (1991), goes so far as to state that participation in voluntary associations is more important than governing, voting, military service, or paying taxes. Kymlicka and Norman in their article "Return of the Citizen" observe that according to civil society theorists, it is through "churches, families, unions, ethnic associations, cooperative, environmental groups, neighborhood associations, women's support groups, charities," that the "virtues of mutual obligation," are learned. It is through participation in these organizations that one learns to become and function as a good member of society (Kymlicka 1994, 364). Participation, voluntary participation in community organizations, is a way of both learning to be a good member of society and of showing civic virtue. It is part of being a good American.[35]

Robert Putnam in his article and then book of the same title, *Bowling Alone*, has written on the decline of participation in all forms of social association in America (Putnam 1995, Putnam 2000). Putnam bemoans the decline in participation in clubs, civic organizations, religious groups, and even bowling leagues. Putnam writes,

> . . . most Americans no longer spend much time in community organizations— we've stopped doing committee work, stopped serving as officers and stopped going to meetings. (Putnam 2000, 63)

Putnam argues that this decline in participation, both in informal social contacts and formal civic forums, damages the social connectedness, the social capital of American society. Even if Putnam is correct regarding the decline in participation in social organizations, overall his writings support rather than diminish the argument presented here regarding the importance of participation in voluntary associations. Putnam is not challenging the importance of participating in voluntary associations. He strongly supports such participation and in fact teaches the existence of a societal need for this participation. Putnam fears the consequences of the decline in sociality and spends nearly a third of his book describing the consequences and proposing solutions to recreate social capital.[36] In sum, even if participation in voluntary associations is presently in decline, it is still regarded as a virtue; it is still regarded as something Americans should do.

Participation in the Political/Electoral Process

T. H. Marshall wrote, "If citizenship is invoked in the defense of rights, the corresponding duties of citizenship cannot be ignored" (Marshall 1973, 123). Often spoken of as a right, it is often overlooked that voting and participation in the electoral process is an obligation of citizenship which builds and strengthens connections between an individual and the broader community. Mary Ann Glendon writes of this in her book *Rights Talk*. She finds it disquieting that the new generation places so much emphasis on personal happiness while failing "to perceive a need to reciprocate by exercising the duties and responsibilities of good citizenship" (Glendon 1991, 128). Specifically, Glendon is amazed that so few young people mention voting as one of the characteristics of good citizenship.

Etzioni, in his book *The Spirit of Community*, who also matches rights with responsibilities, specifically mentions participation in elections. He writes:

> Individuals' rights are to be matched with social responsibilities. If people want to be tried before juries of their peers, they must be willing to serve on them. If they want elected officials that respond to their values and needs, they must involve themselves in the primaries in which the candidates are chosen. (Etzioni 1993, 249)

Etzioni goes on to quote William F. Buckley as referring to the act of voting as a "civic sacrament" (ibid., 141).

John F. Reynolds in his work *Testing Democracy*, also emphasizes the importance of voting as a civic act and responsibility. He observes that in the United States, we have defined voting as a civic function rather than a partisan one, and that this is one of the "unique and cardinal features of the electoral system of the United States" (Reynolds 1988.

173). Janoski in his chapter "Reconstructing Obligations and Patriotism" lists 1) voting and participation in politics and 2) being informed and exercising the franchise wisely, as two political obligations of citizenship (Janoski 2000, 55).

Viewing participation in the electoral process as an obligation of members of the American community is not a new concept. At the beginning of the 20th century, during the Americanization movement, writers often included voting among the responsibilities of citizenship. In 1924, the Hepners observed in their book *The Good Citizen* that "Good citizens take an active part in the election of public officials." They specifically went on to state that "voting for candidates for public office is a right and a privilege of the highest order." Beyond being a privilege, they reminded their readers, "It is also a duty" (Hepner 1924. 319). Mrs. Reginald De Koven, in her work *A Primer of Citizenship* wrote that it was the responsibility of good citizens to be voters who would choose good officers to uphold laws that were just (De Koven 1923. 37). Broome in 1926 wrote in his work *Conduct and Citizenship* "that voting is not only the right but the duty of every good citizen" (Broome 1926. 362).

In 1948, the American Heritage Foundation published a booklet which detailed nine promises of a good citizen. Among these promises were the promise to "vote at all elections," and to inform oneself on the "candidates and issues . . . .' (American Heritage Foundation 1948, 71).

The importance of participating in the political process is dramatically underscored by the verbiage the Supreme Court has used describing situations in which the opportunity to participate in the process has been denied. For example, in the Supreme Court decision commonly referred to as the *The Ku Klux Cases* 110 U.S. 651 (1884), the majority opinion of the Court noted that the selection of the executive and legislative branches were essential to the successful working of our government, and labeled it a dangerous evil to try to unjustly control access to the voting process [110 U.S. 651, 666-667]. In *South Carolina v. Katzenbach* 383 U.S. 301 (1966) the court referred to unjust control over who could vote as an "insidious and pervasive evil" [383 U.S. 301, 309]. The wording used by the Court in these decisions, is declaratory of the essential role of voting and participation in the electoral process to the successful working of government.

Of course voting is not the only manner in which individuals can participate in the political process. Other methods include:

> working either for pay or as a volunteer for a party or candidate for office; signing petitions relating to public issues; attending public meetings or rallies in support of a candidate; writing a letter, telephoning, or telegraphing an editor or public official to express concern about issues; wearing a campaign button or displaying political materials on one's car or residence; and contributing money to political causes. (Wrinkle 1996, 14)

Although voting in congressional or presidential elections is of course limited to individuals who are citizens, volunteering for a party or candidate, assisting in petition drives, attending public meetings or rallies, etc., can be done by either citizens or non-citizens and therefore are appropriate measures of participation which can be used in examining the NLIS respondent population which consisted of both citizens and non-citizens.

Learning English Sufficient to be Able to Participate in the Political Process

Learning English has often been noted as one of those things immigrants need to do to truly become American. Often, English has been included as part of the curriculum inculcating new immigrants into the American way of life. Hartman notes that in 1907, the YMCA taught English language classes along with "the requirements of naturalization, the nature of American government, and something of the background of the new country into which [the immigrant] had come" (Hartman 1967, 28). At about this same time period, Dr. R. DeWitt Mallary at the American International College was also teaching recent immigrants English along with American history and ideals, American government, patriotism, sanitation, and personal hygiene (ibid. 30-31). The belief was that learning English would result in the immigrant having a better overall understanding of the American way of life and would eventually lead to the immigrant incorporating the ideals and aspiration of native-born Americans.

More recently, Gordon listed language, along with social rituals, as qualities immigrants must obtain to be considered American (Gordon 1964, 63). Bellah argues that the erosion of a common language, is "a symptom of the erosion of common meaning," in society (Bellah 1975, x). Thus, Bellah would argue, it is important for immigrants to learn English in order for them to maintain (and by implication understand) the "common meaning" in American society. Glazer agrees with Bellah and also links the adoption of English by new immigrants with the learning of American political principles (Glazer 1996, 87).

In contrast to the perceived unity engendered by immigrants adopting English, Citrin, Hass, Muste, and Reingold note, in their article "Is American Nationalism Changing?", that the "demand" for linguistic diversity on the part of current immigrants has "sparked insecurity about national cohesion and fostered a movement to designate English as the Official language of the United States" (Critin, et.al. 1994, 19). Whether an immigrant's failure to learn English would in fact hamper him from feeling more American is not the principal issue that Citirin, et. al., are raising here. Their point is that other Americans perceive immigrants to be less American if they do not learn English. As an expression of this view, Citrin, et. al., cite a February 1988 California Poll in which 60% of the respondents opposed the "principle underlying the bilingual ballots mandated by law and agreed that "citizens" who can't read English shouldn't be allowed to vote" (ibid.). What the respondents here appeared to be expressing was their opinion that knowledge of English, at least sufficient to complete a ballot, was a minimum criteria they expected of individuals who sought to participate politically in that manner.

The decision to include the ability to speak English as an obligation of being a "true" American for the purposes of the analysis conducted here is strengthened by the results to questions asked in the National Election Study (NES) and the General Social Survey (GSS) in recent surveys. In 1992, the National Election Study (NES) included the question:

> Some people say that there are certain qualities that
> make a person a true American. Others say that there
> isn't anything that makes one person more American
> than another. I'm going to read some of the things that

have been mentioned. For each of the following, tell me how important you think it is in making someone a true American -- extremely important, very (important), somewhat (important), or not at all important.

One of the items mentioned was "Speaking English." The response frequencies to this item are reported in table 2.

Table 2. How Important is Speaking English to Making Someone a True American.

Extremely important	688	*30%*
Very important	845	*37%*
Somewhat important	541	*23%*
Not at All important	221	*10%*
Don't know	9	*< 1%*
No answer	9	*< 1%*
Total	2313	*100%*

(National Election Studies 1992)

This same issue was raised in the 1996 GSS. The question there was:

Some people say the following things are important for being truly American. Others say they are not important. How important do you think each of the following is . . . To be able to speak English?

As reported in table 3, 70% of respondents rated being able to speak English as very important.[37]

Table 3. How Important is Being Able to Speak
English to Being Truly American.

	1996	
Very important	956	*70%*
Fairly important	290	*21%*
Not very important	69	*5%*
Not important at all	25	*2%*
Can't choose	11	*1%*
No answer	16	*1%*
Total	1367	*100%*

(General Social Survey 1996)

In 1992, 1996, and 1998, the NES and GSS alternated in asking a question regarding making English the official language of the United States. The question posed to respondents was:

> Do you FAVOR a law making English the official language of the United States, meaning government
>
> business would be conducted in English only, or do you OPPOSE such a law?

As table 4 displays, the percent of respondents who favored making English the official language of the U.S. has increased modestly between the two NES surveys from 63% in 1992 to 67% in 1998 with little change between 1990 and 2000.[38]

Table 4. Percent of Respondents who Favored Making English
Official Language of the United States.

	1992 NES		1994 GSS		1998 NES		2000 NES	
Favor	1419	*63%*	890	*60%*	853	*67%*	1202	*67%*
Neither	154	*7%*	137	*9%*	70	*5%*	130	*7%*
Oppose	627	*28%*	391	*27%*	353	*28%*	446	*25%*
DK	47	*2%*	50	*3%*	4	*<1%*	24	*1%*
NA	8	*<1%*	6	*<1%*	1	*<1%*	2	*<1%*
Total	2255	*100*	1474	*100*	1281	*100*	1804	*100*

(General Social Survey 1996, National Election Studies 2000)

The 2000 GSS also asked respondents whether they agreed or
disagreed that "Speaking English as the common national language is
what unites all Americans." The results illustrated in table 5 below show
overwhelming support for this proposition.

Table 5. Speaking English as a Common National
Language is what Unites Americans.

	2000	
Strongly Agree	354	25%
Agree	670	48%
Disagree	285	20%
Strongly Disagree	37	3%
DK	45	3%
NA	7	1%
Total	1,398	100%

(General Social Survey 2000)

Certainly these few questions on these two topics are only simple measures for a complicated issue and should not be considered the final statements on this question. However, given that the majority of the respondents in both the GSS and the NES, felt that being able to speak English was a criterion of being truly American, and they favored English as the official language for conducting government business, it does appear that an expectation is being expressed. The GSS and NES respondents appear to be expressing an expectation that those individuals who wish to interact with the government should be able to do so in English. The respondents in these surveys seem to be saying that some level of English competency is a legitimate requirement for those who would function in the American system, or in other words, for those who wish to be considered fully or "truly" Americans.

Conclusion

America is a nation which as been built through immigration. Through
the course of its history, however, America has struggled with the
question of just what it means to be an American. At different times,
different standards have been used to determine who qualified as truly
American. Throughout most of its existence, the ascriptive criteria of
ethnicity, race, and culture have been used to judge whether individuals
would be considered truly and fully American. In contradistinction,
America has also historically had a strong liberal and inclusive approach
which eschewed ascriptive criteria for defining who is an American.
Although this tension has existed for all of America's history, since the
Civil War and the passage of the Fourteenth Amendment, Supreme Court
decisions have increasingly supported the non-ascriptive, more inclusive
approach to defining who is an American. Today, as a result of Supreme
Court decisions, ethnicity, race, and culture can no longer be used as
defining criteria for who is an American.

What has remained constant throughout America's history is a belief
that affirmation, loyalty, and adherence to certain political principles,
obligations, beliefs, and behaviors is what makes an American an
American. Particularly noteworthy in discussions regarding the
obligations of Americans, especially new immigrants becoming
Americans, are two principal obligations. These are:

1. having a belief in the American system of government as
   demonstrated by belief in the American style of republican
   democracy, and belief in the American notions of equality
   and self rule, and

2. living a moral civic life, specifically by

   a. promoting the welfare of the community especially
      through volunteerism and participation in
      voluntary organizations for the good of the
      community,

   b. participation in the political/electoral process, and

    c.   learning English sufficient to be able to participate in the political process.[39]

Having developed these minimum criteria of what it means to be an American, the next step is to operationalize these criteria using questions from the NLIS. With the criteria operationalized, we can then examine the two groups of respondents in the NLIS study, those who saw themselves as Americans and those who saw themselves as members of their home country, to determine if one group is really more "American," than the other.

CHAPTER 3

Logistic Examination of the Allegiance Variable

Through the discussion in the previous chapter, four criteria were developed to create a minimum definition of what it means to be "American." Those four criteria were 1) belief in the American system of government, 2) participating in voluntary organizations, 3) participation in the political/electoral process, and 4) learning English sufficient to be able to participate in the political process.

The question before us now is as follows: are these criteria of being American predictive of national self-identification (American or country of origin) among National Latino Immigrant Survey (NLIS) respondents? This is to say, if we operationalize the criteria developed in the previous chapter using variables from the NLIS, would those variables be predictive of whether NLIS respondents identified themselves as Americans or as a member of their countries of origin?

The objective of this chapter will be to answer this question using the twofold approach of first operationalizing the four criteria using variables from the NLIS, and second conducting a logistic regression using the national self-identification variable from the NLIS as the dependent variable, and the items used to operationalize the four criteria as the independent variables.

The results of the logistic regression analysis will show how well these variables predict whether a respondent identifies as an American or with his country of origin. The hypothesis proposed at the beginning of this paper was that respondents' statements of national self-identification were not political, and hence there would likely be no connection between an operationalized definition of being American and a respondent's national self-identification. If the four criteria are not predictive of national self-identification, this would support the hypothesis that the statements of national self-identification are not political in nature.

Although the national self-identification question was not the primary focus of the NLIS, the NLIS data is nevertheless useful for several reasons. First, the sample drawn for the NLIS was a national sample with appropriate representation from the different Hispanic sub-populations. Second, as noted in the introductory chapter, the sample was drawn specifically of legal immigrants who had been in the U.S. five or more years, thus being qualified to apply for citizenship. Lastly, and also noted in the introductory chapter, the question of national self-identification is specifically asked in the NLIS.

This chapter will proceed by examining the four criteria raised in chapter two in the following order:

- first, participation in voluntary organizations,

- second, participation in the political/electoral process,

- third, learning English, and

- lastly, belief in the American system of government

This order was selected so as to examine the criteria from least complex to most complex. Each criterion will be developed in turn by:

- first reviewing the questionnaire items from the NLIS which relate to each criterion, and

- second, developing scaled items as necessary for each of these points.

After this development, a logistic regression model will be run with the national self-identification variable as the dependent.

NLIS Variables Matched to Criteria for Being an American

Participation in Voluntary Organizations

The literature review in chapter 2 uncovered the importance placed by many writers and scholars on participating in voluntary organizations as part of "being American." The NLIS asked respondents regarding their participation in nine different types of organizations. They were asked whether they were members of a:

- church,

- labor union,

- PTA,

- sports club,

- senior citizens club,

- fraternal order, such as the Masons,

- political organization,

- social club, or

- social club whose members are mostly of the respondents home country.

A summary variable for participation in voluntary organizations was created by summing the number organizations in which a respondent claimed membership.

Participation in the Political Process

Participation in the political process was another point identified as a key component to being "American." The NLIS has two sets of items which apply to this point. The first set of items addressed the respondents' participation in a variety of political activities; the second set of items addressed the respondents' participation in a variety of elections.

Political Participation

The first set of items, which shall be referred to as political participation, focus on participation in the political process in ways other than voting. These items asked respondents whether they had ever participated politically in the United States by:

- following politics in the news,

- writing letters,

- distributing leaflets,

- canvassing or marching,

- attending fund raisers, or contributing money, or

- helping people register or vote.

As with memberships in community organizations, a summary variable was created by adding together the number of activities in which each respondent participated.

Voting

The second set of variables concerning political participation are those which deal specifically with registering to vote and actually voting.

Respondents were asked if they:

- were registered to vote,

- had voted in the 1984 presidential election,

- had voted in the last state election,

- had voted in the last local election, or

- had voted in the last school board election.

The summary variable here was created by giving respondents one point if they were registered to vote, and an additional point for each election in which they had voted.

Learning English

The NLIS asked a total of 8 questions regarding the respondents' ability and use of English . Because language ability and language preference are different concepts, the NLIS asked a set of questions addressing each concept. It is also appropriate to analyze their impact on national self-identification separately.

Language Ability

The NLIS asked respondents 4 questions regarding their English language proficiency. These questions asked respondents to self-assess their ability to:

- understand spoken English,

- speak English,

- write English, and

- read English.

Respondents could answer that they performed these tasks "very well," "well," "not well," or "not at all."

In order to develop a composite score to assess a respondent's English language ability, respondents were given positive or negative points depending on their responses to each item. A respondent received:

- 2 points for an answer of very well,

- 1 point for an answer of well,

- -1 points for a response of not well, and

- -2 points for an answer of not at all.

Thus, if a respondent indicated they 1) understood, 2) spoke, 3) wrote, and 4) read English very well, they would receive a composite score of 8. Conversely, if they indicated they did not do any of these things at all, they would receive a score of -8.

Language Preference

The NLIS also asked four questions dealing with language preference of the respondents. They were asked:

- what language they spoke at home,

- in which language they read the newspaper,

- in which language they listened to the radio, and

- in which language they watched television.

Response categories for each question were English, both, or Spanish. Additionally, for the questions regarding reading the newspaper, listening to the radio, or watching television, the respondents could answer that they did not participate in that particular activity. In creating a composite score for the criterion, respondents were given a score of:

- 1 for each answer of English,

- 0 for each answer where the respondent indicated they used both English and Spanish, or where they indicated they did not participate in that activity, and

- -1   for each answer of Spanish.[40]

Thus, a respondent could receive a maximum score of 4 if they responded that they used English in all four settings. Conversely, a respondent would receive a score of -4 if they replied that they used principally Spanish for all of these activities.

Belief in the American System of Government

In seeking to operationalize the concept of belief in the American system of government, it quickly became apparent this concept would be the most complex to describe from the NLIS data. Unlike the other measures developed above, (participation in community organizations, political participation, voting, language ability, and language preference) the NLIS had no clear set of variables designed to measure belief in the American system of government. However, several questions and groups of questions were included in the NLIS which can be used to show the respondent's familiarity with the American government, and their desire to be part of the American system. Further, some questions inquire about actions respondents may have taken to become part of the American system. Taken together, these variables provide as reasonable an approximation of belief in the American system of government as can be derived from the NLIS data.

Below is a listing of the variables in their different groupings which will be used to operationalize this concept.

Familiarity with American Government

Although certainly not as exact a measure, the NLIS respondents' familiarity with or attention to American politics can be tested by using two variables. These are:

- being able to correctly give the name of the Vice President, and

- Being able to correctly give the name of the governor of their state.

These two variables were grouped together into a single scale which for the sake of convenience will be referred to as "knowledge of government," with the respondent receiving a score of 2 if they responded correctly to each item, a 1 if they responded correctly to only 1 item, and a 0 if they gave no correct response.

A Desire to Be Part of the American System

Three questions fell into this category, and were amenable to grouping into a summary variable. These questions were:

- how important was it to the respondent to become a citizen,

- how important were the following reasons for becoming citizens:

- citizenship allowing them to vote in U.S. elections, and

- citizenship allowing them to participate more equally in American life.

These three questions were already similarly scaled, which allowed them to be combined into a summary variable in which they received 4 points for each item if they answered "very important," 3 points if they answered "somewhat important," 2 points if they answered "not very important," and 1 point if they answered "not at all important." Thus a respondent could receive a maximum score of 12 if they responded "very important" to all three of the above questions.

Reasons for Not Becoming a Citizen

Interestingly, the NLIS included a series of questions asking how important certain reasons were for not becoming a citizen. Three of these items lent themselves for inclusion in this study. These items were:

- they wanted to maintain political ties with their home country,

- they would feel disloyal to their home country, and

- they saw no real benefits to becoming citizens.

Because these questions address very different reasons for not wanting to obtain U.S. citizenship it was important to assure that they were in fact measuring the same attitude. This was done by conducting a reliability analysis and obtaining a Cronbach's alpha score. Cronbach's Alpha essentially indicates how well a set of variables measure a single unidimensional latent construct (UCLA Academic Technology Services 2000). The Cronbach alpha score of .8466 indicates that the three variables are clearly measuring the same attitude.

As with the three variables above, respondents were given between 1 and 4 points for each item, depending on their answers.[41] One point was given for a response of "not at all important," and 4 points were given for a response of "very important."

Actions Taken to Become Part of the American System

Three questions from the NLIS are used to operationalize this topic. The first question was whether the respondent had ever sought to obtain an application for citizenship. Respondents were given a score of 1 if they had ever sought to obtain an application for citizenship, or they were given a score of 0 otherwise.

The other two questions that fall into this category of taking actions to become part of the American System are:

- whether the respondent had studied English since coming to the United States, and

- whether the respondent has ever studied U.S. history or government since coming to the United States.

These two questions were grouped into a single summary variable in which the respondent receiving a score of 2 if they answered they had studied both English and U.S. history/government, a score of 1 if they had studied only one or the other, and a 0 if they had studied neither.

Summary: Belief in the American System of Government

These five variables, knowledge of government, importance of citizenship, reasons for not getting citizenship, getting an application for citizenship, and studying for citizenship were selected to be used together to operationalize belief in the American system of government. As noted above, and as is clear from our discussion thus far, these concepts are coming from several different sections within the NLIS. Since these questions are not coming from sets of questions that were designed to work together, such as the language ability or language preference variables previously described in this chapter, a legitimate question to ask is whether the variables selected to operationalize belief in the American system of government truly group together. Two different tests were used to examine how well these items group together. The first test was the scale reliability test, Cronbach alpha. The Cronbach alpha score for the five variables used for this concept was .3700. Although the value here is not as high as it was for the variables measuring reasons for not being a citizen cited above, it is nevertheless within an acceptable range.

An additional manner of showing that these items group together is through the use of factor analysis. Placing these five variables in a factor analysis yielded a single factor, indicating that they do group together. As noted in table 5, the first factor accounts for 38.784% of the variance.

Table 5. Factor Analysis Results

Com-ponent	Initial Eigenvalues			Extraction Sums of Square Loadings		
	Total	% of Variance	Cum %	Total	% of Variance	Cum%
1	1.939	38.784	38.784	1.939	38.784	38.784
2	.972	19.441	58.226			
3	.848	16.967	75.193			
4	.690	13.792	88.985			
5	.551	11.015	100.000			

The component matrix (see table 6) shows the factor loadings for each of the five variables.

Table 6. Factor Loadings

Know Government Leaders	.590
Importance of Citizenship	.274
Reasons for not getting Citizenship	-.705
Tried to Get Citizenship Application	.748
Studied English or U.S. History/Government	.677

The variable with the lowest factor loading is the summary variable measuring the respondents answers regarding the importance of obtaining citizenship. However, with a factor loading value of .274, it still merits inclusion.

The results from both the reliability analysis and the factor analysis indicate that although these variables came from different sections of the NLIS, they nevertheless do group together and, therefore, can be used as a group to operationalize belief in the American system of government as described above.

Control Variables

Beyond using the variables described above, it is appropriate to use a series of control variables for different demographic characteristics of the NLIS respondent population. Among the variables available in the NLIS that can appropriately serve as control variables are:

- gender,

- age,

- the number of years the respondent has been in the U.S.,

- whether or not the respondent is a citizen,

- income, and

- the number of years of education completed.

The Logistic Regression

Having operationalized the four criteria developed in the previous chapter with items from the NLIS, we are ready to proceed to the logistic regression. The advantage of using logistic regression for this analysis is that it is specifically designed for the examination of dichotomous dependant variables. Unlike linear regression which uses ordinary least squares (OLS) to estimate regression coefficients, logistic regression uses maximum likelihood estimation (MLE) to calculate logit coefficients. In OLS, the objective is to minimize the sum of squared distances between the observed data and the predicted data. In MLE, the objective is to maximize the log likelihood: a reflection of how likely it is (the odds) that the observed values of the dependent variable can be predicted by the observed values of the independent variables.

maximize the log likelihood: a reflection of how likely it is (the odds) that the observed values of the dependent variable can be predicted by the observed values of the independent variables.

With the independent variables constructed as described above, the logistic regression equation was entered as follows:

National Self-Identification = β_0 + β_1 (Gender) + β_2 (Age) + β_3 (Years in the U.S.) + β_4 (Citizenship) + β_5 (Income) + β_6 (Education) + β_7 (Importance of Citizenship) + β_8 (Tried to get Citizenship Application) + β_9 (Reasons for not becoming a Citizen) + β_{10} (Studied English, History/Government) + β_{11} (Memberships in Community Organizations) + β_{12} (Voting) + β_{13} (Political Participation) + β_{14} (English Language Ability) + β_{15} (Language Preference)

Overall, the model was significant with a χ^2_{22df} = 192.929 significant at p = .0000. The model correctly predicted national self-identification in 68.07% of the cases. The model was somewhat more successful in predicting when the respondent's national self-identification was their country of origin (72.43%) than when the respondent's national self-identification was the U.S. (63.35%).

An alternate way of analyzing the model's ability to predict the dependant variable is to calculate the proportional reduction of error (PRE) which provides an estimate of the amount of error recovered by the model. Two measures of PRE are Lambda-p and Goodman/Kruskal's (G/K) Tau-c.

Lambda-p is an asymetrical measure which takes only the row marginal of the non-modal category into account when measuring PRE. It is therefore more sensitive to tables where the data is very unevenly distributed. Goodman and Kurskal's tau-c examines both the row and column marginals in computing PRE and is hence somewhat more robust. In this case both measures give similar approximations of PRE. The Lambda-p value was .3353, and the G/K Tau-c value .3604.

Table 7. Logistic Regression Results - Full Model

Variable	Coefficient (S.E.)
Gender	-.0688 (.1444)
Age	-.0151 (.0062)**
Years in the U.S.	.0297 (.0093)***
Citizenship	.1406 (.3009)
Income	
Income (1)	-.4999 (.3430)
Income (2)	-.3472 (.3050)
Income (3)	-.5054 (.3049)
Income (4)	-.4886 (.3388)
Income (5)	-.5298 (.2874)
Income (6)	-.3604 (.3115)
Income (7)	-.1808 (.3481)
Education	-.0273 (.0203)
Importance of Citizenship	.2698 (.0480)***
Tried to get Citizenship Application	.2668 (.1576)*
Reasons for not becoming a Citizen	-.0510 (.0358)
Studied English, History, or Government	-.0738 (.1016)
Knew Government Officials	-.0923 (.1027)
Memberships in Community Organizations	-.1084 (.0576)*
Voting	.0446 (.0673)
Political Participation	-.0618 (.0743)
English Language Ability	.0096 (.0224)
Language Preference	.2353 (.0403)***
Constant	-1.9475 (.7409)
Number of Cases	1068
Percent Predicted Correctly	68.07%
Proportional Reduction of Error	
Lambda-p	.3353
G-K Tau-c	.3604
	$\chi^2_{22df} = 192.929$
	significant at .0000

* p ≤ .10, ** p ≤ .05, ***p ≤ .01

An examination of the regression results revealed some clear strengths and weaknesses in the ability of different variables to predict national self-identification. Among the variables which showed particular strength were the variables measuring the Importance of Becoming a Citizen (β = .2698, p = .0000), and Language Preference (β = .2353, p = .0000). Two other variables were also significant at the p ≤ .05 level; Age of the Respondent (β = -.0151, p = .0153) and the Number of Years the Respondent Had Been in the U.S. (β = .0297, p = .0014).

Two additional variables had a significance levels at p ≤ .10. The first was Memberships in Community Organizations (β = -.1084, p = .0596), and the second was whether or not the Applicant had Tried to Get an Application for Citizenship (β = .2668, p=.0904).[42]

At the other end of the spectrum, several variables were noteworthy for their lack of significance. Four variables had significance levels of p > .6. These were Gender (β = -.0688, p = .6336), Citizenship (β = .1406, p = .6404), English Ability (β = .0096, p = .6692), and Income (.6927).[43]

Although the results of this first regression provided significant insight into the relative strength of each of the independent variables in predicting national self-identification, it was felt that it would be worthwhile to try and obtain a more parsimonious model. To this end, additional models were run using a backward elimination process using the Likelihood-Ratio statistic as the selection criterion.

The backward elimination process begins by including all independent variables in the model. At each step, each variable is iteratively removed and the likelihood-ratio statistic is calculated by dividing the likelihood for the test model by the likelihood for the model from the previous step. The variable with the highest p value for the likelihood-ratio test is eliminated at each step. Since the parameter estimates for each variable are affected by what other variables are included in the model, re-running the model produces somewhat different results with each iteration. The backward selection process continues until all remaining variables have significant Likelihood-Ratio statistics below a predetermined p value . For this study, the standard significance level for selecting variables in this manner was used. Iterations were continued until all the remaining variables had a value of p ≤ .10.

Allowing the backward elimination process to proceed in this manner generated eleven steps in the selection process. The final model, the model in which all variables had a log LR value of .10 or lower is given below:

National Self-Identification $= \beta_0 + \beta_1$ (Age) $+ \beta_2$ (Years in the U.S.) $+ \beta_3$ (Importance of Citizenship) $+ \beta_4$ (Reasons for not becoming a Citizen) $+ \beta_5$ (Memberships in Community Organizations) $+ \beta_6$ (Language Preference)

The reduced model was significant with a $\chi^2_{22df} = 180.095$ significant at $p = .0000$. The model correctly predicted national self-identification in 66.39% of the cases, as compared to 68.07% of the cases for the full model.

As with the full model, this reduced model (see table 8 below) was somewhat more successful in predicting when the respondents identified with their country of origin (71.53%) than when the respondents identified with the U.S. (60.82%). Using this model, the Lambda-p and G/K Tau-c values are not only similar to each other, but very similar to the Lambda-p and G/K Tau-c values from the original model: the Lambda-p value being .3002 and the G/K Tau-c value being .3267. Although the reduced model was modestly less effective at predicting a respondent's national self-identification overall, it nevertheless compares favorably to the full model and is clearly more parsimonious.

Table 8. Logistic Regression Results - Reduced Model

Variable	Full Model Coefficient (S.E.)	Reduced Model Coefficient (S.E.)
Gender	-.0688 (.1444)	
Age	-.0151 (.0062)	-.0149 (.0056)***
Years in the U.S.	.0297 (.0093)	.0343 (.0089)***
Citizenship	.1406 (.3009)	
Income		
Income (1)	-.4999 (.3430)	
Income (2)	-.3472 (.3050)	
Income (3)	-.5054 (.3049)	
Income (4)	-.4886 (.3388)	
Income (5)	-.5298 (.2874)	
Income (6)	-.3604 (.3115)	
Income (7)	-.1808 (.3481)	
Education	-.0273 (.0203)	
Importance of Citizenship	.2698 (.0480)	
Tried to get Citizenship App	.2668 (.1576)	
Reasons for not Becoming a Citizen	-.0510 (.0358)	-.0770 (.0209)***
Studied English, History or Government	-.0738 (.1016)	
Knew Government Officials	-.0923 (.1027)	
Memberships in Comm. Orgs.	-.1084 (.0576)	-.1157 (.0521)**
Voting	.0446 (.0673)	
Political Participation	-.0618 (.0743)	
English Language Ability	.0096 (.0224)	
Language Preference	.2353 (.0403)	.2314 (.0315)***
Constant	-1.9475 (.7409)	-2.5638 (.5533)
Number of Cases	1068	1068
Percent Predicted Correctly	68.07%	66.39%
Proportional Reduction of Error		
Lambda-p	.3353	.3002
G-K Tau-c	.3604	.3267
	$\chi^2_{22\ df} = 192.929$	$\chi^2_{6\ df} = 180.095$
	significant at .0000	significant at .0000

** $p \le .05$, *** $p \le .01$

An examination of the regression results shows that variables measuring the Importance of Becoming a Citizen (β = .2750, p = .0000), and Language Preference (β = .2314, p = .000) continue to be highly significant. Similarly, the variables of Age (β = -.0149, p = .0073), Years in the U.S. (β = .0343, p = .001), and Memberships in Community Organizations (β = -.1157, p = .0263) continue to be significant.

The variable indicating whether or not the respondent had "Tried to Get a Citizenship Application", which was marginally significant in the original regression, was eliminated from the equation in the 11th and last step. The significance level for this variable rose above the p = .10 limit in the 10th step when the Education variable was dropped. Although initially puzzling, the connection between these two variables might be understood in the following manner. If the variable, "Getting an Application for Citizenship", was measuring not only the desire to become a citizen, but also the capacity to challenge the immigration bureaucracy, then there would be a possibility of a modest co-linear relationship with education. Individuals with a higher level of education might be more capable of challenging the bureaucratic hurdles of obtaining citizenship, and hence more likely to obtain an application. It should also be remembered, however, that Education, although only significant at the p = .1781 level, did have a negative β coefficient (-.0273).

The variable "Reasons for Not Becoming a Citizen" was not significant in the full model, however, interestingly it was retained in the model selected through the backward elimination process. It dropped below the p $\leq$ .10 level (β = -.0770, p = .0002) in the 3rd step when the Citizenship variable was eliminated. That the Citizenship variable was eliminated this early in the backward selection process is reflective of its lack of predictive ability. Nevertheless, it was apparently acting as a suppressor variable. The relationship between the two variables is clear, in that those who had become citizens obviously had no reasons for not becoming citizens.

Discussion

As described in the previous chapter, the academic literature, political figures and commentators, and Supreme Court decisions have established concepts of what it means to be an "American." The objective of this chapter was to operationalize those concepts using variables from the NLIS and then use those variables in a logistic regression to examine if they could predict whether respondents in the NLIS viewed themselves as "American" or as members of their countries of origin.

What we have seen is that of the ten variables used to operationalize the concepts developed in the previous chapter, (not including the control variables) only two, the summary variable used to measure importance of being a U.S. citizen, and the language preference variable, were significant at the $p \leq .05$ level in the full model. Additionally, the variables measuring respondents' feelings about reasons for not becoming a citizen and the variable measuring memberships in community organizations became significant in the model developed through the backward elimination procedure. In either model, the ability of these variables to predict identification with the U.S. is somewhat lower than their ability to predict identification with the respondent's country of origin.

In addition to the variables listed above, two control variables, Age of the respondent and Years in the U.S. were significant in both models.

Upon initial examination, perhaps the bigger surprises come not from what items are good predictors of national self-identification, but rather from which items were not good predictors. It would be expected that the longer respondents had been in the U.S. the more likely they would be to identify themselves as Americans. Similarly, it is not surprising that those who prefer to use English in different settings are more likely to identify themselves as Americans. What is initially surprising is that variables such as Citizenship or Education are not good predictors. In the case of Citizenship, it must be remembered that obtaining citizenship is a function not only of desire and purposeful intent, but also of opportunity, confidence to challenge the immigration bureaucracy, ability to pass the exam, etc. Nevertheless the relationship between Citizenship and national self-identification will be something to watch closely in the focus group interviews. As for Education, an assumption that greater education would automatically associate an individual to American culture is not necessarily correct. As was noted in the previous chapter, Stanley Lieberson (1985) and Tom Smith (1980) both found that it was individuals with lower levels of education who were less likely to identify themselves with a hyphenated ancestry. Thus, although greater education might facilitate an individual's functioning in the United States, greater education may also make them aware of their own heritage. It is, therefore, understandable that education would not be a good predictor of national self-identification.

More puzzling, however, was the negative relationship between "Number of Memberships in Community Organizations" and national self-identification as American. Putnam (2000) as well as others cited above, argue strongly that participation in community organizations is an American characteristic. The possible answer to this apparent inconsistency is not to be found in the data available through the NLIS, but rather through the comments given by some of the participants in the focus groups which will be discussed in the next chapter.

Summary

Given the results of the logistic regression, how predictive were the original four concepts developed in the previous chapter to the actual national self-identification of the NLIS respondents? The results are certainly mixed. On the one hand, variables such as the summary variables on the "Importance of Citizenship", or "Reasons for Not Becoming a Citizen" give support to the connection between the concept of belief in the American system of government and national self-identification as an American. Conversely, Voting or "Participation in Politics" were not predictive at all.

English language ability was among the poorest predictors. Conversely, English language preference was one of the strongest predictors. The original concept developed in the previous chapter was that a requirement of being American was that immigrants should develop English language ability sufficient to be able to participate in the political process. From the logistic regression results it is apparent there is a conceptual disconnect between English language ability and preference for using the English language. The results indicate that those who prefer to speak Spanish are more likely to identify with their countries of origin, and that increased English language ability does not increase the probability of their identifying as Americans.

Table 9. Logistic Regression Summary

Concepts	NLIS Variable(s)	Significant
Belief in the	Importance of Being a	YES
American System of	Citizen	YES
Government	Reasons for not being a	NO
	Citizen	NO
	Tried to get Application	NO
	Studied English/History	
	Knew Government Leaders	
Memberships in	Memberships in Community	YES
Community	Organizations	(negatively)
Organizations		
Political	Voting	NO
Participation	Political Participation	NO
Learn English	English Ability	NO
sufficient to	Language Preference	YES
participate in the		
political process		

If we were to redefine Language Preference as an expression of cultural preference rather than as a marker of American identity, the difference between the two variables is easier to understand. Further, this would support the proposal that national self-identification is more of a cultural expression, rather than a political one.

In theory, those respondents who displayed more of the characteristics of being "American," as outlined in the previous chapter, should have been more likely to identify with the U.S.; whereas those respondents who displayed fewer of those characteristics should have been more likely to identify with their countries of origin. However, what we have found is that most of the criteria developed in the previous chapter do not predict national self-identification in the NLIS data set.

This leads us back to the initial question of this study. If respondents' self-identification as Americans or with their countries of origin is not adequately predicted by the criteria for being "American" found in academic literature, political commentary, and popular writings, what then are Hispanic immigrants expressing when they identify themselves as American, or with their countries of origin? This question clearly cannot be fully answered through an inquiry into the NLIS data, but rather calls for in-depth interviews specifically designed to address this issue. This, then, is the next step.

CHAPTER 4

Talking to the People:
The Focus Groups

Background

The statistical analysis of the data from the NLIS provided some insight into what variables were or were not related to whether immigrants identify themselves as Americans or with their countries of origin. Unfortunately, the analysis of the NLIS necessarily suffers from two limitations. First, as was noted in the previous chapter, the NLIS questionnaire was not developed specifically to address the question of national self-identification. Therefore even a thorough secondary analysis of the NLIS data can be expected to leave some aspects of the national self-identification issue unexplored. Second, being a telephone survey, the NLIS researchers had the opportunity to receive input from a large number of respondents. However, the telephone survey format makes it very difficult to explore issues in depth. Consequently, feelings and explanation as to why respondents answered questions in a certain manner and often not collected. Perhaps the most important piece of information which could not be addressed in the NLIS was what respondents actually meant when they expressed identification as Americans or with their countries of origin.

In this study, this limitation was addressed by gathering information via focus group interviews conducted with participants selected from a population similar to that of the NLIS.[44] Focus groups, as a research method, have the strength of 1) allowing for exploration and discovery, 2) providing context and depth, and 3) providing a context for the "why" behind respondents' answers. (Morgan 1998, 1:12). In contrast to the telephone survey methodology used in the NLIS, which asked a wide range of brief questions from a large sample of respondents, a focus group interview approach asks a few probing open-ended questions of a necessarily small number of participants. As noted by Morgan, "focus groups produce large amounts of concentrated data in a short period of time" (ibid., 1:32). In a focus group interview, a moderator can explore in greater depth the feelings of the focus group participants with regard to an issue. Focus group interviews allow participants the opportunity to more completely express their opinions.

For this study, the information gathered through focus groups will:

- provide confirmation and clarification for the results of the logistic regression,

- allow respondents to answer for themselves what they mean when they identify themselves as Americans or with their countries of origin, and lastly

- explore additional issues which could not be addressed via the logistic regression.

Focus Group Organization

Unlike sampling for survey research or experimental designs, which attempts to obtain a representation of a large population by selecting a statistically valid sample of respondents, selecting participants for focus groups has a different goal in mind. Focus groups are designed to provide greater depth of information on specific topics of interest, therefore, sampling for focus groups is purposive in nature (Morgan 1998, 2:56), and participants are selected according to the goals or needs of the project. Thus, Morgan notes, participants can or should be selected according to the categories of participants which need to be heard and what kinds of similarities and differences need to be examined (ibid., 64).

Focus Group Participant Selection Criteria

Because the purpose of the focus group interviews was to provide greater depth to the quantitative analysis done on the NLIS data, the population selected for the focus groups mirrored as much as possible the population of the NLIS study. The population invited to the focus group interviews were adult Hispanic immigrants who had been legal residents in the U.S. for five or more years, living in areas of high, moderate, and low Hispanic concentration. The areas initially targeted were: Huntington Park, California; Riverside, California; Salt Lake City, Utah; and Provo, Utah. The Huntington Park locale was selected to provide Hispanics from an area of high Hispanic concentration. The Riverside site was selected to provide Hispanics from an area with somewhat lower Hispanic concentration, but still within a state with a very high Hispanic presence. The Salt Lake City and Provo sites were selected to provide participants from areas of lower local Hispanic concentration as well as from a state where the Hispanic presence overall is significantly lower.

Because the logistic regression indicated that the age of the respondent and time in the U.S. were significant variables in predicting national self-identification, these factors were also taken into consideration in recruiting participants for the focus group interviews.

Participant Selection

Initially a three stage process was planned for recruiting participants. Key individuals were going to be contacted in each area where the focus groups were to be held. These key contacts were asked to provide a list of four to five additional names of individuals in each of these areas. This second set of individuals were then to be asked to provide the names of three to four individuals each. It was to be this third set of individuals which would then be screened for participation in the focus groups.

The intent of this three stage process was two-fold. First this method would assure that individuals selected for the focus group were not known to the researcher. Second, this method was expected to aid in diversifying the pool of participants.

Almost immediately, a minor revision was required. The selected key individuals in the different areas largely felt it improper to pass along the responsibility of recruiting persons, but rather preferred to do the recruiting themselves, further, insisting that the gatherings take place in their homes. As I discussed the organization of the focus groups with several of the key individuals, it became apparent that their requests were based upon and in keeping with notions of propriety and familiarity within the Latino culture. After ensuring that the two goals of the selection process would be met (selecting individuals not known to the researcher, and selecting a diverse pool of individuals), the selected key individuals were permitted to organize the groups in the manner they suggested, and conduct the groups in their homes.

In Salt Lake City a different kind of recruitment opportunity presented itself. A residential neighborhood near the down town area hosts a Hispanic community and education center known as The Guadalupe Center. Among its many activities, this center sponsors evening classes for members of the local community. Discussions with the Center director and his designated staff members revealed both an enthusiasm to assist in the project, as well as a ready list of individuals who could be screened for eligibility and interest to participate in the focus groups. After again ensuring that the two goals of the selection process would be met, Guadalupe Center personal were invited assist in organizing the focus group in the Salt Lake area.

Because the opportunity presented itself, and as an extra measure to assure the desired diversity among the recruited population, the number of groups was increased resulting in interviews being conducted in the following locations:

- Salt Lake City, Utah

- Bell Gardens, Los Angeles County, California, [45]

- Riverside, Riverside County, California

- Rialto, San Bernardino County, California

- Chino, San Bernardino County, California

- Provo, Utah

Language of the Focus Groups

Approximately 71% of the respondents to the NLIS indicated they spoke principally Spanish in their homes. An additional 19% indicated they spoke both English and Spanish equally in their homes. Given that this study was tapping into a population similar to the NLIS, it was expected that the majority, if not all, of the participants in the focus groups would be comfortable discussing these issues in Spanish. Nevertheless in each focus group it was made clear that participants should feel comfortable in using the language in which they felt most comfortable. Also, all the written materials used during the focus groups were provided in both English and Spanish.

Only two of the participants (Frank - Bell Gardens, Mike - Chino[46]) spoke exclusively in English, although both understood Spanish. Several of the participants switched between Spanish and English occasionally during the course of the discussion. This was usually done to clarify a point or because a term could not be recalled in Spanish. As a focus group moderator with over ten years of experience conducting focus groups in English, Spanish, and bilingually, these groups presented no particular or peculiar difficulties.

Short Questionnaire

In order to obtain some minimal demographic information, and some information which could be useful in comparing the focus group participants to the NLIS respondents, a short questionnaire was distributed to the focus group participants. This questionnaire replicated a subset of questions from the NLIS.

The questionnaires were translated using the following method:

- An initial translator made a translation of the questionnaire from English into Spanish.

- A second translator verified the translation. Where changes were suggested, I acted as arbiter determining which of the two suggested translation would be used.

- Last, a third translator reviewed the Spanish translation comparing it back to the English original.

Tape Recording the Focus Groups

The focus group interviews were audio tape recorded for the purpose of supplementing the notes taken by the facilitator. The focus group participants were made aware that they were going to be recorded and were asked to give their consent in writing. Participants were advised that if at any point during the focus group they would like to make a comment with the tape recorder turned off, they could request the recorder to be turned off. No one expressed discomfort at being recorded, and it did not appear to affect the openness of the interviews in any way.

Identification of Participants

The nature of focus group interviews is such that being able to call participants by name during the course of the interview may significantly add to a positive, friendly, open atmosphere. Therefore, it is appropriate to know and use the first name of the participants during the course of the focus group. It is not necessary, however, to know or record the last name of a participant.

Even though only first names were used, all notes, survey instruments, and tapes were secured as confidential materials. Since the project plan required the taping of the focus group only for the purpose of supplementing the facilitator's notes, a full transcription of the tapes was not required, and therefore no transcriptionist was employed. This further added to the confidentiality of the taped materials.

Informed Consent

All potential participants were informed that participation in the study was completely voluntary, that audio recordings of the session would be made, and that their names would never be used in reporting the results of the study. Participants were informed that they could refuse to answer any question, that they could request to have the tape recording stopped while they gave a particular answer, and that they could cease participation in the focus group at any time. Written consent forms, in the language of their choice, were distributed to each of the study participant. Each consent form reiterated the voluntary and confidential nature of the study.

Direct Benefit/Risk to Participants

Although participants in this study did not receive any direct benefit as a result of their participation, they were informed that their participation would aid in broadening the understanding of immigrant attitudes about becoming American.

Despite the offering of any incentive for participation, all of the participants seemed very happy at the opportunity participate in an academic endeavor, and became very engaged in the process. Several participants indicated that they had never had the opportunity to have this type of in depth, thoughtful discussion on these types of issues.

Because all of the participants were legal immigrants, by identifying the participants only by their first names, and by securing all the materials as described above, the participants were not placed at risk by participating in this study.

Participant Demographics

A total of 52 individuals participated in 6 focus groups. As expected, the majority of the participants identified Mexico as their country of origin, however, there were also participants from El Salvador, Guatemala, Nicaragua, Argentina, Bolivia, and Peru. Below are brief comparisons between the focus group participants and the NLIS respondents on the variables used as control variables in the logistic regression reported in the previous chapter.

Gender

Forty-six percent of the focus group participants were male and 54% female. This compares to the 39% male and 61% female composition of the NLIS respondents Although there is clearly some difference here between the two populations, the results of the logistic regression indicated that gender was not significant in predicting the national self-identification variable. This finding was verified through the focus group interviews in that there was no discernable difference in the responses given by males and females on any of the questions.

Age

The focus group interview participants ranged in age between 21 and 65 with a median age of 38. By comparison, the NLIS population ranged from 18 to 88 with a median age of 40.

Years in the United States

As with the NLIS study, participants in the focus groups represented a broad range of years of residency in the United States. Focus group participants had been in the U.S. between 5 and 46 years with a median of 16 years in the U.S. By comparison, the NLIS population ranged between 1 and 58 years in the U.S. with a median of 18 years in the U.S.[47]

Citizenship

Fifty-five percent of the participants in the focus groups were citizens. Among NLIS respondents, only 36% were citizens. As with gender, citizenship as a variable was not significant in the logistic regression. This finding was confirmed in the focus groups in that, with a few exceptions which will be noted later in this chapter, there were no discernable differences in the responses of citizens and non-citizens to the questions asked during the focus group interviews.

Income

Income level for the participants in the focus group interviews ranged from the lowest category - less than $750 a month, to the highest category - more than $5,200 a month. The median category was $2,501 to $3,000 a month. In the NLIS study, the income ranged between its lowest category of less than $500 a month ($736 in adjusted 2000 dollars), to its highest category of over $3,000 a month ($4,415 adjusted). Its median income category was $1,201 to $1,499 a month ($1,767 to$2,206 adjusted). A higher median income level of the participants in the focus group interviews than in the NLIS population is largely due to composition of the group in Chino. This group had 6 respondents with incomes over $5,200 a month, and no respondents with incomes less than $3,401 a month. Although participants in this group were clearly more economically advantaged than those in the other groups, it should be remembered that, as with gender, the results of the logistic regression indicated that income was not significant in predicting the national self-identification variable. This finding was verified through the focus group interviews in that there was no discernable difference in the responses given by the Chino group and any of the other groups.

Education

The education levels of the focus group participants and NLIS respondents were very similar. The focus group participants had a median education level of 12 years of completed schooling whereas the NLIS respondents had a median education level of 11 years. The focus group participants had a mean education level of 11.31 years of completed schooling and the NLIS respondents having a mean education level of 10.07 years.

Interview Questions

Given that the purpose of conducting focus group interviews was to better understand the responses given in the NLIS survey, there was an obvious need to allow respondents time to fully express their answers. Perhaps one of the biggest errors made in conducting focus group interviews is to ask too many questions and not allow sufficient time for participants to elaborate upon their responses. For example, if a focus group consisted of 8 persons, and was scheduled to last 90 minutes, asking a series of 10 questions would allow each respondent just over 1 minute to answer each question. This would likely not be sufficient time for a participant to fully explain their answers, nor would it allow time for discussion among participants, or probes by the focus group moderator. With this in mind, these focus groups were planned to run 12 to 2 hours with 5 principal questions being asked. This would allow each respondent in an 8-person group 2.5 minutes to respond to any question, plus still provide time for some amount of follow-up probing, as well as time for a brief welcome and a few close-ended introductory questions at the beginning of the session.

During the welcome, the purpose of the focus group was explained[48], and the informed consent forms were distributed to and signed by the participants.

Introductory Questions

The introductory questions included:

- What is your country of origin?

- At what age did you immigrate to the U.S.?

- How long have you been in the U.S.?

Understanding that age might be a sensitive topic for some of the participants, the questions were usually asked with the word "approximately" added to the age or years in the U.S. question. This allowed the possibility for participants to not give their exact age if they felt uncomfortable doing so. The actual impact on the groups, however, was that rather than discomfort, this became a joking point as they made comments such as, "Oh, now we are going to know how old you really are!" The overall effect was that this allowed the participants to come together as a group, and to shed some inhibitions about talking and sharing as a group. It effectively became a great ice breaker.

Principal Questions

Five principal questions were asked of the focus group participants. These questions were:

- Which of the following best describes how you see yourself:
  More as an American, more as a member of your country of
  origin, or as something else?

This question automatically elicited discussion by the participants as
to why they viewed themselves the way they did.

- To you, what is an American or what does it mean to be
  "American"?

This question provided the participants an opportunity to express their
feelings about what it means to be American, but also why they did or did
not identify themselves as American in the previous question.

The next principal question was:

- Have you sought to obtain U.S. citizenship? If yes why, if
  no, why not?

This question brought into the discussion an apparently political
question, that of citizenship. As will be reported below, however, often
citizenship turned out not to be a political issue.

The final questions were as follow:

- If the border were to close tomorrow and you would have to
  either stay here or stay in your country of origin; where
  would you choose to stay?

- Imagine a situation where the U.S. has become involved in a
  war with a European country. If asked, would you fight for
  the U.S. or encourage your children to fight for the U.S.?
  What if it were a Latin American country other than your
  country of origin? What if it were your country of origin?

Focus Group Results

The following sections will summarize the comments from the focus group participants on the principal questions. Although names will be used in reporting out the results of the focus group, it must be understood that these are pseudonyms and not the true names of the participants. The pseudonyms have been very purposefully selected so as to convey much of the same contextual information that the participant's real name would have conveyed. For example, comments from an individual named Juan who identifies himself as an American might take on a different tone to the reader if he were a John and who identified himself as an American. Therefore, if a participant had a Spanish name such as Pedro, the pseudonym replacement similarly became a Spanish name such as Carlos. In turn, a participant with an English name such as John would receive pseudonym such as Charles. Multiple derivations of the same name, such as Pedro, Peter and Pete among the pseudonyms reflect similar derivations in the true names of the participants. If multiple participants share the same pseudonym it is because they shared the same true name. Where multiple participants had the same name, they are differentiated by location of interview.

Which of the Following Best Describes how You See Yourself: More as an American[49], More as a Member of Your Country of Origin, or as Something Else?

As anticipated, this was not an easy question for most of the participants to answer. Those who identified with the United States usually made comments such as those of Peter (Rialto) who said that at work, he felt American. Daniel (Bell Gardens) stated he felt totally American because it (America) had given him so much. Gilbert (Provo) said he felt American, and added that when he woke up in the morning, he didn't expect that anyone was going to treat him as a Bolivian. He didn't feel segregated by his heritage. Manuel (Riverside) although interestingly not using the term "American" said he was from here, after all, his house, his family, and his dog were all from here. There were a few respondents who had grown up on the border, or in towns in Mexico where there was a strong American corporate presence. The comment from Hortencia (Riverside) typifies their feelings. She said she had grown up on the border, but had always felt as though she were from the U.S.

But those expressing identification with the U.S. often had mixed feelings about their identity. Peter (Rialto), for example, after saying he felt American, went on to say that it was when he was with his people (Mexicans) that he felt a conflict. Sometimes, he mused, he wished he could feel more Mexican. Alberto (Chino) indicated he felt American, but it depended on how he was seen by others. Alberto related that when he had encountered racism on the part of the government it made him feel more Mexican.

This confusion was certainly also felt by many who identified with their countries of origin. Isaac (Bell Gardens) indicated that if someone asked him, "what are you" he would reply Salvadorian. But, he went on to say, he had grown up American. On the street he eats American food; at home, of course, he eats Salvadorian food. Frank (Francisco - Bell Gardens) wryly stated that when he looks in the mirror in the morning, he sees a Mexican. Interestingly, Augie had been in the U.S. over 30 years, preferred to speak English, and spoke English without an accent. Cristina (Riverside) expressed the feeling of many when she said that she was a Mexican, but her life was here now. She indicated that she'd like to visit but not return to Mexico. Simply, from her point of view, there are more opportunities here. But, she concluded, "I like this country."

There were a few individuals, who like Pablo (Salt Lake) indicated he felt Mexican, but went on to say they felt at home here, because this land, the American West, was really part of Mexico illegally acquired by the U.S. As far as José was concerned, he was very comfortable living here in the midst of his language (Spanish), his culture (Mexican), his family and friends. Given this strong association to his Mexican heritage, I was somewhat surprised to find out a little bit later in the interview, that Pablo was a naturalized U.S. citizen.

Bertha (Provo), also a naturalized citizen identified herself as Mexican. She said you never lose your roots. Being a naturalized citizen "no me quita el nopal!" Bertha stated emphatically.[50]

Apart from those who identified themselves as Americans or with their countries of origin, there were many who could not classify themselves with either group. Antonio (Salt Lake) expressed the feeling of several participants when he said that his roots were in Mexico, but he was here now so he guessed that made him Mexican American, but really he was from neither here nor there anymore.

Overall, the most common threads through all of the comments, both from those who identified as Americans and those who identified with their countries of origin, was that the United States offered great opportunities to progress financially and educationally. The U.S. offered a home, a place where their families could grow, and a new culture. As Rosa-2 (Riverside) stated, she considers herself Mexican, but all she has or ever will have is from here in the U.S. Pedro (Riverside) expressed his feelings by saying that undoubtedly they were all from Mexico, but as they absorb U.S. culture, they become American. He went on to say that as he travels home (to Mexico) he doesn't feel comfortable any more. He's Mexican, but he feels American. He said, "I've absorbed the culture."

Consistently, the participants spoke about the love they held for the cultures of their countries of origin, and many commented on the families still living there.[51] Although references were often made to, "mi país," which could be translated "my country," I believe that in the context of their other comments the more appropriate translation would be, "my homeland."

There were no political references made at all when expressing any identification with the United States. The most common political references were the negative references made toward their nations of origin. Sonia-1 (Chino), Juan-1 (Chino), and Pete (Chino) all agreed that the only reason they were in the U.S. rather than in Mexico was because of government corruption there.

To You, What is an American or What Does it Mean to be "American?"

The responses to this question fell along four basic lines of thought. Participants defined being American:

- using ethnic/racial concepts,

- using cultural concepts,

- as a mind set, and

- as a set of political values.

The first line of thought was that an American was an Anglo-Saxon or Gavacho (white American). Among those defining American this way was Rosa-3 (Riverside) who noted that her kids were born here, but they were not really Americans, because to be an American you had to be white. Alberto (Chino) said Americans are the Anglo-Saxons, the white Europeans, and also the minorities (Blacks) here in the U.S. Rosa-1 (Riverside) put it bluntly by answering that Americans were the Gringos. When Alicia (Bell Gardens), a naturalized citizen, returned to the U.S. from a trip to Canada, she was stopped at the border and asked to declare citizenship. But stating she was American was not sufficient, they questioned her further as to where she was born. Alicia said it was because she didn't look American. She wasn't white.

The second line of thought was that "American" referred to a particular culture. It's eating hamburgers instead of beans, was how Magdalena (Rialto) described it. Isaac (Bell Gardens) also defined being American in terms of culture. He referred to the ideas and customs that make Americans Americans. Isaac and others also spoke about the clothing and mannerisms they identified as being American. After all, Jorge said, America is a melting pot, so being American had to be more than just race. It was this sense of culture that caused Hilda (Bell Gardens, a naturalized citizen, to declare she could never call herself American because her roots were in Mexico. Manuel (Riverside) felt that when immigrant children lose their native language and adopt English, they become American. Jorge (Riverside) immediately added that it was not just language, but culture as well.

Salvador (Rialto), however felt that being American went beyond culture. To be American, Salvador said is to feel what Americans feel; to understand what gives them joy, what they consider fun. Salvador, a naturalized U.S. citizen, didn't feel that this was something he had achieved. Frank (Francisco - Bell Gardens) described being American as a mind set. Elvia (Provo) also described being American as a mind set, specifically mentioning attributes such as being logical and organized. Although a naturalized citizen, Elvia frankly admitted that she didn't have what she described as Anglo-Saxon attitudes. Juan-2 (Chino) felt that being American was a way of looking at things, a set of values. Gilbert (Provo) also felt being American was a mind set, but he described it in more detail. He felt being American as being able to live within the American system; being able to dealing with the culture and the laws.

There were some participants who specifically mentioned political values as the values that make someone American. Jorge (Chino) spoke of being American as having freedom of speech and liberty. To him an American is someone who feels that liberty. Daniel (Bell Gardens) spoke of the freedom to vote, the freedom to move about, the freedom to act, and the freedom to exercise your rights. Eljia (Chino) talked about adapting to the American System. When you've adapted, then you are an American she said. Edgar (Bell Gardens) expressed the feelings of some when he bluntly stated that when you become a citizen, then you are an American.

Clearly, there was then no consensus on what it meant to be an American. The four themes that developed, beyond being different in focus, also describe a range of attitudes about the very possibility of an Hispanic immigrant ever becoming American. Those who viewed being American in ethnic/racial terms were also saying that it was impossible for them ever to become Americans. As Alberto (Chino) put it, "I'm not going to look whiter because I'm in the U.S. longer."

For some who viewed being American in cultural terms, the possibility existed of becoming American. For example Peter (Rialto) who said he felt American at work, even though he wished he could be more Mexican. However, there were those who viewed their roots as a permanent attachment to their country of origin which meant they would never become American, even if they became citizens. This was the case with Hilda (Bell Gardens) cited above, who was a naturalized citizen. But those who viewed being American in cultural terms at least felt their children could become or were American, which was not a possibility for those who viewed being American in ethnic/racial terms.

Those who viewed being American as a mind set were also divided as to the possibility of becoming American. It was, after all as Elvia (Provo) said, just a matter of being more logical, more organized. However, even she felt that some of those traits were not all positive. Yes, Americans were more logical, but they were also socially cold, not necessarily an attribute to strive for in her estimation. Salvador (Rialto) talked about a shared set of experiences making one American. But, even though he was a naturalized citizen, he didn't yet feel he had obtained this level of shared understanding.

Interestingly, those who defined being American in political terms were potentially the most inclusive. Belief in the American government, being accepting and supportive of the freedoms enjoyed in the United States, accepting civic responsibility, are things that anyone, regardless of race, cultural attachments, or lack of shared experience can nevertheless support and be a part of.

There were, however, some curious aspects to some of these "American" political behaviors that actually may have strengthened the participants identification with their countries of origin rather than as Americans. As noted in the previous chapter's discussion of the logistic regression results, participation in community organizations was negatively correlated to respondents identifying themselves as Americans. Although this was initially somewhat of a puzzle, it was clarified by the comments made in the focus groups. Generally, when the focus group participants spoke of involvement in community organizations or even voting, they spoke of them as opportunities to give voice to the needs of their families, the Hispanic community or as opportunities to benefit their people. One of the principle reasons Alicia (Bell Gardens) became a citizen was so that she could be in a better position to help Salvadorian refugees. She related her experience of going to the Mission in Los Angeles and sleeping alongside the refugees in efforts to thwart INS mass deportations. The literature and the focus group participants agree that community activism are very American things to do, but the reality is that at least to some extent they are being done to give voice to the needs of their families and the broader Hispanic community. Thus, this type of participation may strengthen ties to the ethnic community while at the same time exercising a classic American virtue of civic participation.

Have You Sought to Obtain U.S. Citizenship? If Yes Why, if No Why Not?

As noted above, approximately half of the participants in the focus group interviews were naturalized citizens. The majority of those who were not yet citizens indicated they were in process of seeking to obtain citizenship.

Reasons for Being a Citizen

The reasons for becoming citizens fell principally along five lines of thought, which were:

- they were now resident here so they might as well obtain citizenship,

- citizenship would allow for greater opportunities,

- citizenship would provide a level of security within society no longer available through mere legal residency,

- citizenship would allow for fuller participation in the United States community, and

- citizenship was an obligation of living in the Unites States.

The first line of thought was clearly expressed by Pedro (Riverside) who said that one day he decided he was going to stay in the U.S., so why not become a citizen. Once her husband died, Avelina (Bell Gardens) felt she had no reason to ever return to Mexico. Her family was now here, so she became a citizen.

The second line of thinking was that obtaining citizenship would allow for greater opportunities. Among the benefits mentioned by focus group participants were economic benefits, and the benefits of mobility.

Rosa-3 (Riverside) and Magdalena (Rialto) also felt citizenship was important for the range and quality of jobs that could be obtained. Liliana (Salt Lake) felt all Hispanic immigrants wanted to become citizens particularly for the economic benefits that would come as a result. She also observed that citizenship gave one the ability to move back and forth across the border easily. Alfredo (Salt Lake) concurred that as an American citizen you were free to travel anywhere relatively unencumbered. Alicia (Bell Gardens) commented on how great it was to go past the border stations and say, "American citizen." Javier (Provo) and Bertha (Provo) both commented that a principle reason they had sought citizenship was for the benefit of being able to bring other family members to the United States. This was a very rarely mentioned benefit of citizenship among the focus group participants.

A third line of thinking was that citizenship provided for a sense of security residing in the United States. For these individuals there appeared to be a heightened state of concern because of what they perceived as anti-immigrant feelings and anti-immigrant legislation in the very recent past. Being merely a legal resident was no longer a safe or secure status in the U.S. Comments from Jesus (Bell Gardens) were typical of this group when he said that he felt Mexican, but became a citizen to make a life here, and so as not to have legal problems later. Rosa-1 (Riverside) and Nicolasas (Riverside) echoed these feelings, that obtaining citizenship would provide a greater sense of security. Nicolasa (Rialto) commented that she couldn't go back to El Salvador, so she needed some assurance that she belonged here.

A few individuals viewed obtaining citizenship as an important step in being able to more fully participate in the United States. Salvador (Rialto) stated that citizenship was important to participate in political things. He said he kept hearing of the importance of Latino political participation. He wanted to participate for the benefit of his children. Gilbert (Provo) felt similarly. He observed that becoming a citizen had not been a priority to him until he married and began having children here. Rosa-3 (Riverside) also felt citizenship was important to be able to more fully participate politically and socially in the U.S. Alicia (Bell Gardens) also noted the importance of voting, but she also noted that with dual citizenship, she also voted in Mexico.

Lastly, a few individuals viewed obtaining citizenship as an obligation of living in the U.S. Peter (Rialto) said he felt he was part of this nation. He lived here, and felt an obligation to the nation, and hence wanted to be a citizen.

Reasons for Not Being a Citizen

Not very many individuals gave reasons for not becoming a citizen. Most of the focus group participants who were not citizens were in the process of becoming citizens. Of those who had not yet obtained citizenship the reasons fell along two themes, 1) challenges of obtaining citizenship, and 2) no real desire or benefit to obtaining citizenship.

Angela (Salt Lake), Rosa (Salt Lake) and Antonio (Salt Lake) all mentioned fear of the exam as one reason why they had put off applying for citizenship. Maria (Salt Lake) observed wryly that the individuals born in the United States didn't have to take an exam to be citizens, and she wondered if many of them could pass such a test if it were given. Pablo (Salt Lake), now a citizen, mentioned that for many people, time and money were real roadblocks to obtaining citizenship.

Isaac (Bell Gardens), although he said he felt he had grown up American, felt no hurry to become a citizen. He said rather frankly that he didn't have a need to be a citizen. Frank (Bell Gardens) concurred saying that until he decided that he wanted to vote he really hadn't had a need to become a citizen. Julio (Provo) said he was in no rush to obtain citizenship. After all, he noted, whether you are a citizen, a legal resident, or an illegal alien, you have the rights in the United States. Perhaps the strongest opinion along this line came from Betty (Rialto) who said that to her citizenship was just a piece of paper, a legal technicality. This comment was in sharp contrast to the feelings of Daniel (Bell Gardens) who said that to be an American was a great privilege, or the comments of Rosa-3 (Riverside) who said that on the day she became a citizen she felt different, or Alicia (Bell Gardens) who said that after she became a citizen she felt more American.

Summary

Reasons for being a citizen ranged from almost a default action because they intended to be permanent residents of the United States, to an action taken for the benefits that would be derived, whether those benefits were economic, a sense of security, or a possibility for political involvement, to a sense of obligation. Reasons for not becoming a citizen were either procedural (time, money, etc), fear of passing the test, or simply a lack of interest.

Except for those few like Peter (Rialto) who felt it a sense of obligation to become a citizen, or Rosa-3 (Riverside) or Alicia (Bell Gardens) who felt more American after becoming citizens, becoming a citizen was not necessarily an expression of feeling American. It should be remembered that even Alicia, who said she felt more American after becoming a citizen, still primarily identifies herself as Mexican. This confirms the results of the logistic regression where citizenship was not a good predictor of national self-identification.

If the Border Were to Close Tomorrow, and You Would Have to Either Stay Here or Stay in Your Country of Origin, Where Would You Choose to Stay?

With only two exceptions, all the participants of the focus groups eventually concluded that they would stay in the United States, but the decision was often not an easy one. The opinion of many was well expressed by Bertha (Provo) who said, "Que la sieren, yo me quedo aquí!" (Let them close it, I'm staying here). For others it was a more difficult decision. Avelina (Bell Gardens), Jesus (Bell Gardens), and Hilda (Bell Gardens) all agreed that if it weren't for family here in the U.S., they would return to Mexico if the borders were to close. Angela (Salt Lake) and Antonio (Salt Lake) were the only participants who didn't feel they could answer the question. Pablo's (Salt Lake) quandary was specifically that his family was now all here in the U.S., while much of his wife's family remained in Mexico.

Family was the central theme around which most of the respondents formed their answers to this question. Nicolasas (Riverside) said she would stay here, but with great pain because of the family she would leave in Mexico. But the most common answers are typified by the response of Elvia (Provo) who stated that her children were here, as well as her mother and her brother. Why would she leave? It is worth noting that the fact she is now a U.S. citizen did not appear to enter into her reasons for staying.

Imagine a Situation Where the U.S. Has Become Involved in a War with a European Country. If asked, Would You Fight for the U.S. or Encourage Your Children to Fight for the U.S.? What if it Were a Latin American Country Other than Your Country of Origin? What if it Were Your Country of Origin?

Most participants of the focus groups had little difficulty declaring they would support the United States in a conflict or a war against a European country. Peter (Rialto) expressed the feelings of many when he said that it was an part of citizenship, an obligation.[52] Supporting the nation in such a cause is part of the price of living here. Javier (Provo) felt it was part of his obligation as a naturalized citizen. I would have to go, was his reply. Jorge (Riverside) declared he felt we have to defend what we have here in the U.S. He also felt this was a way of thanking the nation for what it had given him. Jorge (Chino) felt similarly and spoke about what this country had given him. Julio (Provo), although earlier expressing he felt no rush to obtain citizenship, noted with some pride the heritage of Latino's serving in the U.S. military.

When the question was posed about supporting the United States in a war against a Latin American country, the large majority still voiced the opinion that they would fight for the U.S. However, a few individuals now began to express some concerns. Elvia (Provo) for example was honestly surprised that the U.S. had supported England against Argentina in the war for the Maldivas (Falkland Islands). Why, she wondered, would the U.S. support a powerful European country instead of a less powerful county in its own hemisphere? Rosa (Salt Lake) said she would have to take the cause of the war into consideration. Alfredo (Salt Lake) and Antonio (Salt Lake) both wondered if there might not be racial overtones involved. Although these few concerns were raised, overall, the large majority expressed support for the U.S. in a war against a Latin American country.

Not surprisingly, coming to a decision on this issue became much more difficult when the question was asked whether they would support the United States in a war against their own countries of origin. There were many sighs and comments about the difficult nature of the question. Still, most indicated they would support the United States. Isaac (Bell Gardens) said that any country that threatened this country threatened his family, his lifestyle, and his life. Pedro (Riverside) felt it would be very hard, but he had sworn allegiance to the U.S. by becoming a citizen. Jorge (Riverside) at first expressed the feeling that he would fight for whichever country had the just cause. He shortly thereafter recanted and said he would have to fight for the U.S.

The principal problem in fighting against their countries of origin was well expressed by Alberto (Chino) who said he would not oppose the U.S. in a war against Mexico, but he could not fight, not against his family. Pete (Chino) expressed this same concern about fighting against his families in Mexico. He went on to say that he would have no problem fighting against the Mexican government, it was the Mexican people he would not want to fight against. Liz (Chino) voiced the opinion that without reservation she would fight against her country of origin to end the corruption there. Javier (Provo) expressed a similar sentiment saying he would have no problem fighting against Peru, if it were with the intent of annexation.

Alicia (Bell Gardens), a naturalized citizen, said it would be very difficult to fight against Mexico. She expressed the feeling that this was her blood, her history, her religion. Perhaps, she pondered, she might even fight against the U.S. She was joined in this opinion by Hilda (Bell Gardens) and Nicolasas (Riverside)

Perhaps the most poignant remark was made by Salvador (Rialto) who related that he had registered to fight in the Gulf War, but against Mexico, it would be very difficult. He went on to say that if he were asked to fight against Mexico he would go, but, possibly he wouldn't be capable of killing a Mexican, and would simply allow himself to be killed instead.

Summary

The purpose of conducting the focus group interviews was threefold:

- to provide confirmation and clarification for the results of the logistic regression,

- to allow respondents to answer for themselves what they mean when they identify themselves as Americans, or with their countries of origin, and lastly

- to explore issues which could not be addressed via the logistic regression.

The focus groups accomplished these tasks.

The participants in the groups discussed freely, and openly shared their opinions. Although, as noted above, the different questions often prompted differing lines of thoughts among the participants, these lines of thought were consistent from group to group, and were raised by the participants themselves typically in response to only the principle question asked by the moderator.

The focus group interviews were particularly useful in addressing the questions left unanswered by the logistic regression of the previous chapter. The logistic regression raised the question of why there should be a negative correlation between membership in community organizations and identification as American. As reported in this chapter, one reason appears to be that individuals joining groups do so to some extent to represent the Hispanic community and Hispanic interests. As noted above, this action may be an American trait, but may actually serve to strengthen ties to the Hispanic community. That voting was also viewed as a manner of expressing the needs of the Hispanic community, and hence an action which might strengthen ties to the Hispanic community, may also be partially a reason why voting and political participation were not significant variables in predicting national self-identification.

"Reasons for becoming a citizen" was a variable that was significantly predictive of national self-identification in the logistic regression. The reasons used to construct the variable for the logistic regression, a strong desire to be a citizen, a desire to vote, and a desire to participate more fully in American life, were in fact among the reasons mentioned by participants in the focus groups. But there were many other reasons also given for being in the United States, and these reasons were given by individuals who later answered that they would be willing to fight for the United States in an armed conflict. Those reasons could be categorized as the opportunities that the United States has to offer.

But what about the central question of what it means to be an American? As reported above, there were many diverse opinions, but largely, for most of the participants involved, the definitions were not political in nature, and those who identified themselves with their countries of origin were identifying with the cultural aspects of those countries. The comments made by participants indicating their distrust of the governmental systems in their home countries, and even their willingness to fight against the governments of their home countries, made it clear there was no political connection there. This was a consistent theme in all of the focus groups. When they spoke of being in the United States, the participants often spoke of the opportunities this nation afforded them: the opportunities for education, for economic prosperity, and for a better way of life. Only on a few occasions did any of the participants speak of the political freedoms available here. When they spoke of their countries of origin, they spoke of the corruption, the bribery, the lack of government stability. It is most likely that the participants all understood that the prosperity available to them in this country was largely possible due to the political situation here, but the political aspects were not what they focused upon; the political aspects of life in the U.S. were, aside from a few exceptions, never verbalized.

Overall then, when the participants in these focus groups identified themselves as American or from their countries of origin, they were referring to ethnic/racial or cultural concepts, not political concepts. Specifically, those who identified with their countries of origin were identifying with the people and the cultures of those countries, but not with the governments. Conversely, the overwhelming willingness to support the United States in armed conflict speaks to the political loyalty of the majority of the participants in spite of the majority of the participants identifying themselves with their countries of origin.

CHAPTER 5

Conclusions

This research began with the observation of an apparent inconsistency between the behavior of Hispanic immigrants in Miami and Houston and their expressed national self-identification. The inconsistency existed in that individuals who expressed American values and behaviors (a desire to live in the U.S., praise for living conditions here over their countries of origin, a desire to improve their local communities, a desire to participate in politically) nevertheless continued to identify with their countries of origin. This paradox was further observed among respondents to the National Latino Immigrant Survey (NLIS) who, although all legal immigrants to the United States, split almost evenly on a national self-identification question: some identifying themselves as Americans and others identifying with their countries of origin.

This research has provided at least a partial resolution to this paradox. In the introductory chapter it was suggested that the paradox was only a paradox if the statements of identification with their countries of origin made by the individuals in Miami and Houston, and by the respondents to the NLIS were political in nature. It was proposed that perhaps these statements were not political statements at all, but rather cultural in nature. It was further proposed that if a minimum criteria were developed, defining what it meant to be an American, the relationship between that criteria and a respondent's self-identified national identity (American or country of origin) could help determine whether the statements of national self-identity were political or cultural in nature. If the criteria were

129

adequate predictors of national self-identification then the argument that the statements were political would be supported. If, however, the criteria were not adequate predictors of national self-identification, if individuals who fit the minimum criteria of being American nevertheless identified with their countries of origin, then the political nature of their statements regarding national self-identity would be called into question, and it might be suspected that those expressions were expressions of cultural preference instead.

What Is An American

To be able to explore the apparent paradox, it was important first to develop a definition of what is an American. The intent was to use this definition to "test" the NLIS respondents.

As noted in Chapter 2, the definition of who qualifies as American has varied considerably over the years. This is perhaps most clearly demonstrated in the opinions rendered by the Supreme Court over the history of this nation. These decisions clearly demonstrated that although at one time race, ethnicity, or culture were appropriate characteristics for disqualifying individuals from being Americans (*Dred Scott*, *Ping*, *Plessy* etc.). Those criteria are no longer legally acceptable for defining who is an American (*Shelly*, *Brown*, *Loving* etc.). As Wilkinson wrote:

> We stand before the law as equals. Its commands speak
> to the citizen, not to his race. The Anglo American and
> the Hispanic American pay the same taxes and obey the
> same speed limits as the Asian American and the African
> American. (Wilkinson 1997, 83)

Having determined what were not appropriate definitions of being American, the chapter went on to describe concepts that were appropriate criteria. Using the writings of political scholars, political commentators, historical political figures, and Supreme Court opinions, four concepts were proposed: 1) Belief in the American System of Government, 2) participating in voluntary organizations, 3) participation in the political/electoral process, and 4) learning English sufficient to be able to participate in the political process.[53] These criteria were not proposed as an absolute definition of being American, but rather more as describing the minimum threshold of what it means to be an American. The reasoning was that if this definition were going to be used to examine the attitudes and opinions of Hispanic immigrants, then a minimum threshold would serve that purpose. If at this minimum threshold differences were observed between those who identified themselves as Americans and those who identified with their countries of origin, then we could reasonably infer that those differences would exist under more stringent criteria.

The Logistic Regression

Ten variables constructed from the NLIS data were used to operationalize the four criteria developed in Chapter 2. The operationalized criteria were then used in a logistic regression with national self-identity as the dependent variable. As was discussed in Chapter 3, the logistic regression results demonstrated that not all of the criteria developed in Chapter 2 were good predictors of whether respondents in the NLIS would identify themselves as Americans, or with their countries of origin. It was particularly noteworthy that variables such as Citizenship (a control variable), English Language Proficiency, Participation in Political Activities or Voting, and most of the variables associated with belief in the American system of government were not good predictors of national self-identification.

Only four of the variables used to operationalize the criteria from Chapter 2 were statistically sound predictors of national self-identification. Two of the variables which were good predictors (Importance of Citizenship, and Reasons for not Becoming a Citizen) do appear to support the connection between political concepts and national self-identification. However, the same cannot be said of the other variables. Although Language Preference, for example, was a good predictor of national self-identity, the fact that English Language Ability was not a good predictor called into question the validity of using language preference as an indicator of being American. Although these concepts have been used together jointly in past research (Garza 1996) the large disparity in their predictive abilities in this research calls the approach into question, at least when addressing issues of national self-identification. The predictive value of the Language Preference variable may actually then strengthen the argument that the expressions of national self-identification were cultural in nature, particularly when it is remembered that language preference is a key indicator of maintaining culture as noted by Keefe and Padilla (Keefe and Padilla 1987).

Memberships in community organizations, an archetypal American characteristic observed by writers from Tocqueville to Putnam, turned out to be significant, but negatively associated with national self-identification. Thus, NLIS respondents exhibiting more of the "American" characteristic of being involved in community organizations were in fact more likely to identify with their countries of origin, all other variables being held constant. Thus although predictive of national self-identity, it certainly was not predictive in a manner that supports the connection between the developed criteria and national self-identification. Thus only two of the 10 variables used to operationalize the criteria developed in Chapter 2 can be said to be supportive of a positive connection between the developed definition of what it means to be an American, and a respondent's actual self-identification as either an American or a member of their country of origin. Overall, these results would support the hypothesis that the respondents' statements of national self-identification are not political in nature, but rather cultural.

The Focus Groups

The results from the focus groups gave additional support to the hypothesis that the statements of national self-identification among Hispanic immigrants are cultural rather than political in nature. From the focus groups we learned that although some of the respondents thought of being Americans in political terms (Daniel - Bell Gardens, Edgar - Bell Gardens, Elijia - Chino), others thought of being American in terms of it being a mind set (Frank - Bell Gardens, Juan 2 - Chino, Gilbert - Provo, Elvia - Provo). But most described it in either cultural or ethnic/racial terms (Peter - Rialto, Magdalena - Rialto, Hilda - Bell Gardens, Rosa 1 - Riverside, Alberto - Chino, etc.)

Perhaps more important, however, was how respondents described their relationships to their countries of origin. Although clearly referring to their countries of origin with fondness and often longing, it was clear that, other than for the very rare exception, the participants in the focus groups were here in the United States to stay. Beyond merely being here to stay, it was clear that for most they had made a commitment to make this their home, to support their families in adapting to life here, to raise their children here, and to defend this nation through the force of arms if necessary. Comments such as those from Pete (Chino), Liz (Chino) or Javier (Provo) who said they would fight against their home countries not only because of an obligation to the United States, but to overthrow the governments in their homelands are illustrative of the fact that the attachment these respondents felt in identifying themselves with their homelands was not an attachment to the political structure, but rather an attachment to their culture, their people, and their extended families still residing there. Although there were those who, like Alicia (Bell Gardens), indicated they might return and fight with their homelands against the United States, these individuals were again the very rare exception. And even then, the reasoning was not political, as Alicia (Bell Gardens) stated to fight against Mexico would be to fighting against her blood, her history, her religion.

Consistently, it appears that these were the attachments which were most critical to the participants in the focus groups: the attachments of family, of blood, and of culture. So it was not surprising that when participating in community organizations, or even in political participation, it was often done for the benefit of the family and the broader Hispanic community.

As observed at the end of the Chapter 4, when focus group participants spoke about being in the United States, they most often spoke of the opportunities this nation afforded them. Only on a few occasions did the participants speak in political terms. When they spoke of their countries of origin, they only spoke in political terms when mentioning negative perceptions of the government such as the corruption, the bribery, the lack of government stability that existed in their native countries. When they spoke with fondness of their native lands, they spoke of family, friends, culture, and heritage.

Summary

Both the results of the logistic regression and the results of the focus groups support the conclusion that most often when Hispanic immigrants respond to the question of how they identify themselves, they are using cultural not political terms. There are some individuals in the focus groups who viewed being American in political terms in that they value the political freedoms available in the United States, and specifically mentioned their commitment to the U.S. made either implicitly by choosing to reside here, or explicitly by having taken an oath of citizenship. However, in light of the overall findings from the focus group discussion, it would appear that the strongest reasons for Hispanic immigrants identifying with their countries of origin are familial and cultural, not political. The implication here is that when the news shows a demonstration of a Hispanic group here in the U.S. waving flags of their home countries, they are not expressing loyalty to their home country over the U.S., but rather they are expressing their identity as a cultural group within the U.S. Just as marching in a St. Patrick's Day parade does not necessarily express allegiance to Ireland, marching in a Cinco de Mayo parade does not necessarily express allegiance to Mexico.

Suggestion for Further Research

Although there are many areas which might call for additional research, only two will be mentioned here.

First, it is important to remember that both the National Latino Immigrant Survey and this research are cross-sectional in nature and not longitudinal. They are snapshots in time of what is unquestionably a dynamic process. Certainly attitudes in the United States about what it means to be an American have undergone dramatic change in the course of time in which some of the NLIS and focus group participants have resided here. Five of the Supreme Court decisions broadening the definition of who qualifies to be an American have happened in the last 50 years. The Unites States has gone through periods of intense, some might argue virtually paranoid, patriotism with anti-communist feelings, and through periods of self-questioning and questioning of government intent as during Vietnam. Similarly, for ethnic minorities there was a time when there were great efforts were made to appear to be white, as when Blacks used hair straighteners and skin lighteners. Then there came a time when it was not only acceptable to be ethnic, but to some extent it became a symbol of pride or political power (Black is beautiful, Chicano Power, etc.). It would be difficult to imagine that these changing patterns within the broader American socio-politcal culture have not affected and will not continue to affect immigrant attitudes toward their adopted nation. A series of cross-sectional studies will not address this issue adequately. What is truly needed is a longitudinal study with a panel of participants.

Second, Dahl expresses a concern over a situation which he describes as hyper-egoism in which there is a fragmentation and concern for either the individual or for a subgroup of society rather for the whole of society. (Dahl 1996, 9-10). The negative association between memberships in community organizations and identification with the U.S. revealed in the logistic regression, as well as the results of the focus groups might lead to speculation that Dahl's fears are being realized. I do not believe this to be the case, however. Although there are some who clearly view their community as being at odds with the broader community, as the young man who expressed in graphic terms his disapproval of the government's actions in the Elian Ramirez case[54], overall there appears to be a willingness to work within the system and be part of the nation. Nevertheless, this is an area that merits additional research.

Conclusion

In 1996, I received an email from Jerold Pearson, Director of Market Research at Stanford University, in which he gave the following quotation from Kurt Vonnegut's *Mother Night*. "People are insane. They will do anything at any time, and God help anybody who looks for reasons."

In this case, however, we may have found a reason. In the introductory chapter it was stated that the paradox, was only a paradox if the statements Hispanic immigrants made in identifying with their countries of origin were political in nature. The results of the logistic regression and the focus groups would lead to the conclusion that when Hispanic immigrants identify with their countries of origin they are most likely expressing cultural preference, not political identity.

America is a nation built by immigrants. Americans have also historically viewed the newest wave of immigrants with suspicion and concern. Perhaps, this is the next paradox which should be examined.

Footnotes

[1] Both the definition of what it means to be an American, and what the respondents meant in declaring that they had no intentions of becoming "American" are key concepts which will be more fully discussed below.

[2] U.S. Census Bureau, Census 2000 Brief, *Overview of Race and Hispanic Origin*, by Elizabeth M. Grieco, and Rachel C. Cassidy. (Washington, D.C., 2001), 3.

[3] Table ST-EST2002-ASRO-03 - State Characteristic Estimates Source: Population Division, U.S. Census Bureau Release Date: September, 18, 2003

[4] U.S. Census Bureau, Current Population Reports, Series P23-206, *Profile of the Foreign-Born Population in the United States: 2000*, by Dianne Schmidley. (Washington, D.C.: U.S. Government Printing Office, 2001), 24.

[5] U.S. Census Bureau, Current Population Reports, P20-539, *The Foreign-Born Population in the United States: March 2002*, by Dianne Schmidley. (Washington, D.C.: U.S. Census Bureau, 2003), 2.

[6] The most current compiled source of public opinion polling data on this issue is Karlyn H Bowman, AEI Studies in Public Opinion, *America After 9/11: Public Opinion on The War on Terrorism, The War with Iraq, and America's Place in the World*, (American Enterprise Institute, 2004) [on-line]; 154.

[7] See Reginald Horsman *Race and Manifest Destiny*.

[8] Of course, the growth of the immigrant Hispanic population does not in and of itself mean that the paradox will continue. Certainly, each era of immigration has its own peculiar characteristics, and the conditions surrounding the immigrants' arrival in the U.S. also greatly affect the assimilation of the immigrant (Portes and Zhou 1993, 75). However, understanding the factors that have contributed to the existence of this paradox among current Hispanic immigrants could aid us in understanding the paradox, if it exists, among future Hispanic immigrants.

[9] Although it is common to refer to a Hispanic culture, several scholars have questioned the actual existence of a pan-"Hispanic" culture, noting the many differences in the cultures covered under the Hispanic umbrella (Nelson and Tienda, 1985).

[10] The tone of Wilkinson's statement conveys his feelings and concern that this is not a positive change for the makeup of the American population. This concern conveys an assumption that somehow, the post 1790 immigrants are different than, and apparently less desirable than the pre-1790 immigrants.

[11] This question was asked of a national sample of persons 18 or older. There were 1,255 valid responses distributed as follows: 60% good, 34% bad, 3% neither, and 3% not sure.

[12] Survey conducted by Hart and Teeter Research Companies. Telephone interviews were conducted with 1,213 adults. Respondents were asked "When it comes to immigration in the United States, to you think that our country is too open to immigrants from other countries, too closed to immigrants from other countries, or does our country strike the right balance in accepting immigrants from other countries?" Fifty-one percent responded too open, 7% too closed, 37% about right, and 5% indicated not sure (available from Public Agenda Online <http://www.publicagenda.org/issues/ angles_graph.cfm?issue_type= immigration&id=258&graph=pcc5.gif>, [15 March 2000]). It is curious to note that only six months later, Governor Tom Vilsack of Iowa announced an effort to encourage immigrants to settle in Iowa to help boost a declining population (Available at CNN.Com <http://www.cnn.com/2000/US/09/04/iowa.meltingpot.ap/index.html>, [4 September 2000]).

[13] General Social Survey 2000, variable name "letin".

[14] Survey Organization: Gallup Organization, sponsored by CNN and USA Today. On-line available from Public Agenda 2004.

[15] General Social Survey 2000, variable name immunite.

[16] Undocumented residents pose a unique quandary in that they benefit by residence in the community, and they provide benefits to the community, yet they are clearly without the law in their residence status. What could and should be required of them during their tenure in the United States is indeed an interesting question, however, since the data we are using specifically is limited to legal residents, our discussions will also be limited to legal residents.

[17] The Spanish and the French were also encountered during the initial westward expansion, but they are not the focus of this research, and, therefore, will not be included in this discussion.

[18] Lest it be thought that these are attitudes of a past era, it should be noted that in online response to a discussion on immigration on the Provo Herald's web site (Harktheherald.com) an individual posted the following comment on May 24, 2004: "Ever wonder why Mexico is a third world country? Because it's full of Mexicans!"

[19] It is important not to overlook Huntington's inclusion of language and habits (culture) in his list of qualifiers for being American. The use of language and culture as criteria for being American will be discussed later in this chapter.

[20] This was recently illustrated in a discussion I had with a colleague from Texas. I mentioned to him that I had met many Anglo individuals who had immigrated from other states to Texas, and who now considered themselves and were considered by their neighbors to be Texans. I queried him as to whether I, being of Mexican heritage, if upon moving to Texas could ever become considered a Texan. He replied, with some embarrassment, that I could never be a Texan; I would always be a Mexican.

[21] Although not asking specifically about immigrants, results from the 2002 General Social Survey lend additional support to this line of thought. Respondents were asked if members of ethnic minorities must better adapt to the ways of mainstream American culture in order to have a smoothly functioning society. Sixty percent agreed or strongly agreed.

[22] This is interestingly the same basic argument made by authors such as Cubberley and Roberts (cited above) regarding immigrants in the early 1900's.

[23] Although these amendments were theoretically designed to create a more inclusive definition of "American," it is noteworthy that the wording of the Fourteenth Amendment specifies penalties only when "male inhabitants" are denied the franchise. It also continues to exclude "Indians not taxed" from inclusion in the calculations of congressional seat apportionments. Women were not guaranteed the right to vote until 1920, and Native Americans were not "granted" citizenship until 1924.

[24] Justice Harlan in his dissenting opinion commented on the functional effect of the decision in its relation to quasi-state action.

[25] Source: Patrick Air Force Base history page, <http://www.pafb.af.mil/DEOMI/ hisp.htm>, [11 October 2000]. Medal of Honor Statistics available from <http://www.army.mil/cmh-pg/mohstats.htm>, [11October 2000], and World Book Encyclopedia, 1988 ed., s.v. "Vietnam war." See also Department of Defense, Defense Link web site at <http://www.defenselink.mil/, particularly http://www.defenselink.mil/ specials/hispanic/recipients1.html which lists all 37 Hispanic Medal of Honor recipients.

[26] *Plessy*, discussed earlier, was decided after Strauder, but, much to the surprise of some Supreme Court observers, circumvented the Strauder ruling by stating that laws segregating the races did not automatically imply a superior/inferior relationship between the races. Harlan's dissent in Plessy, as previously cited, found this line of reasoning essentially ludicrous.

[27] In *Reitman v. Mulkey*, 387 U.S. 369 (1967), the court continued and expanded this course of action ruling that a California statute giving owners of real property the right to refuse to sell, lease or rent that property to

any person at their discretion violated the equal protection clause of the Fourteenth Amendment.

[28] The Court here is quoting from *Yick Wo v. Hopkins*, 118 U.S. 356 (1886) wherein Justice Mathews giving the majority opinion for the Court writes, "The case of the political franchise of voting is one. Though not regarded strictly as a natural right, but as a privilege merely conceded by society, according to its will, under certain conditions, nevertheless it is regarded as a fundamental political right, because preservative of all rights" [118 U.S. 356, 370].

[29] A modest example of this might be the reaction of the Cuban community to the INS intervention in the Elian Gonzalez case. After Elian was forcibly removed from his Great Uncle's home in Miami, in compliance with instructions from the U.S. Attorney General, demonstrators on the street expressed their outrage at the federal government. One demonstrator in his wrath shouted, "F*** this country!" He was placing the desires of his community above his loyalty to the nation. It is also important to note, however, that although there is in this community great Cuban solidarity, it is loyalty to a Cuba that does not exist outside of the boundaries of the United States.

[30] The questioning of an individual's loyalty to country is a serious matter, and great caution should be taken that investigations deal with issues of loyalty, not race or ethnicity. The activities of German-American clubs prior to World War I in which they openly supported Germany against France and Britain, was a clear cause for political concern. On the other hand, the Korematsu case in World War II, cited above, did not consider political loyalty at all, only race.

[31] Conversely, Americans were much less likely to mention pride in the physical characteristics of the American people, physical features of the nation, or national contributions to the arts as compared to members of these other countries. In the introduction to this book we raised the possibility that NLIS respondents were expressing cultural preference rather than political allegiance when they indicated identification with countries of origin. These results support this possibility. If citizens of other countries identify first with cultural or other aspects of their nations rather than with their political systems, it suggests the possibility that immigrants to the U.S. when expressing

identification to their countries of origin are, in fact, expressing identification with the cultural aspects of their native countries.

[32] See also James W. Prothro and Charles M. Grigg "Fundamental Principles of Democracy: Bases of Agreement and Disagreement" *Journal of Politics* 22 (February 1960): 282-86, Herbert McClosky "AConsensus and Ideology in American Politics," *American Political Science Review* 58 (June 1964): 365-68. Devine, *Political Culture*, pp. 179-230, and Frank R. Westie, "The American Dilemma: An Empirical Test," *American Sociological Review* 30 (August 1965): 531-32.

[33] Interestingly he uses B.H. Roberts, Representative from Utah as an example. Specifically he notes that even though Roberts was a member of Congress, he was still only allowed to have one wife, clearly a reference to earlier polygamist Mormon practices. More than merely an interesting side note, this indicates that Brewer's definitions of good character were based on traditional Christian concepts.

[34] By nobility here Dahl means selflessness.

[35] Janowitz does note a particular problem in recognizing voluntary associations as a civic virtue, however. He contends that given an expectation of political advocacy in democracies, some differentiation must be made regarding the extent to which voluntary associations are seeking rights, privileges, or benefits as opposed to seeking the public welfare (Janowitz 1980, 16-17). For this analysis, given that both political participation and showing concern for community welfare are viewed as positive "American" traits, then participation in a voluntary association with either political or community interests in mind qualifies as an indicator of being American.

[36] Although there are those who believe that Putnam's measure of civic engagement is incorrect, they are not in disagreement as to the importance of civic engagement, which is the point being made here.

[37] This question has not been repeated in the General Social Survey.

[38] The 2000 General Social Survey also asked respondents regarding making English the official language of the United States, but only offered two response categories, Favor or Oppose, thus that variable is not directly comparable on this table.

[39] For ease of reference, these four points will hereafter be referred to as four criteria and will subsequently be listed as: 1) belief in the American system of government, 2) participating in voluntary organizations, 3) participation in the political/electoral process, and 4) learning English sufficient to be able to participate in the political process.

[40] The rationale for this scaling is based on the concepts of the importance of learning and using English as a marker of being American developed in the previous chapter. Thus, if an individual prefers to use Spanish for one of the listed activities, it could be interpreted as a negative indicator to their being American. Conversely, if they prefer to use English, it could be interpreted as a positive indicators to their being American. If the respondents indicate they use both languages, they have been given a zero score because the use of both languages does not clearly indicate a preference toward or away from being American. Similarly, if the respondents indicate they did not participate in a particular activity, it is scored as a zero because their non-participation in that activity provides no measure of preference on that item toward or away from being American by this definition.

[41] The items here are phrased in such a manner that a score of 4 reflects greater identification with country of origin, whereas a score of 4 on one of the previous questions reflected a greater identification with the U.S. It would not be unusual in such situations to reverse the coding of the responses so that positive numbers always reflected greater identification to the U.S. However, allowing the items to retain their original coding actually makes them more easily read and understood in the factor analysis and logistic regression results. In these procedures the original coding produces negative values, which is exactly what is expected when the name of the variable is read.

[42] Two levels of income were also significant at the $p \leq .10$ level. These were income level 3 - \$801 to \$1200 a month, and income level 5 – \$1,500 to \$2,000 a month. Overall, however, the income variable had a significance level of $p = .6927$.

[43] Because Income was entered as a categorical variable, SPSS calculates no overall β value. See table 7 for the β values for each of the income categories.

[44] As previously noted, the respondents in the NLIS were legal Hispanic immigrants who had been in the United States for five or more years.

[45] Bell Gardens has a concentration of Hispanics very similar to Huntington Park. This group included participants from Huntington Park, Bell Gardens, Commerce, East Los Angeles, Central Los Angeles, and Montebello.

[46] These are not the real names of the participants. The discussion of how pseudonyms were selected for the respondents is given in the section entitles Focus Group Results below.

[47] A variable for "years in the United States" was not part of the original NLIS data set, but rather was calculated by subtracting the respondent's year of immigration from 1988, the year of the survey. Using this method of calculation, four individuals in the data set appear to have been in the United States less than five years. This would appear to violate the inclusion criteria for the NLIS that respondents have been in the U.S. for 5 or more years. However, a provision in the screening questions allowed individuals who had "been married for three years or more to someone who has been a U.S. citizen for three years or more," to participate in the study. In all four cases in question, the individuals were or had been married, and given their inclusion in the data set I assume the original study appropriately qualified them, and hence they were not eliminate from this examination.

[48] During the recruitment process, all of the participants had been informed as to the nature and purpose of the focus group. In effect, this was a re-explanation and clarification of the project and gave the participants an opportunity to ask any questions they might have had about the purpose of the focus group interviews.

[49] An interesting and important issue was raised by members in five of the six groups regarding the phrasing of this question. It was pointed out by at least one person in each of the five groups, whereas from the point of view of individuals in the United States, being American is synonymous with being from the United States; outside the U.S. many individuals identify anyone from the either the North or South American continents as being American. Three individuals, one each in Salt Lake, Chino, and Provo, expressed what could be fairly described as feelings of indignation that residents of the U.S. had misappropriate the term "Americans" to refer to only themselves to the

exclusion of other nations on these continents. Having anticipated this possibility, I was prepared to diffuse the issue by agreeing the usage was technically incorrect, but stating that for the purposes of this study, we could agree to use the common usage. Everyone quickly agreed.

[50] "No me quita el nopal" literally means - it doesn't remove the cactus from me. This is a reference to the heritage symbol of the cactus emblem on the Mexican flag. This is not an expression of political loyalty to the Mexican flag, but rather to the Mexican culture. The English idiomatic equivalent would be to say, "you can take the boy out of the country, but you can=t take the country out of the boy."

[51] Often, when drawing some link to the U.S., participants made comments about their children having been born or being raised here.

[52] Although the word citizenship was specifically used, the feelings seemed to imply residency in the U.S., and not exclusively citizenship.

[53] It is an interesting observation that three of these four criteria were manifest by the individuals interviewed in the pre-study focus group interviews in Miami and Houston: 1) belief in the American system of government as manifest by their decisions to immigrate and obtain legal residence in the United States, 2) an expressed desire to participate in community affairs, and 3) and expressed desire to participate politically to improve their communities.

[54] Disapproval of government action is certainly not limited to the Hispanic community. Others with very disparate points of view, such as Vietnam era protestors or pro-life demonstrators, have forcefully and sometimes violently disagreed with the government's official position on various issues.

Bibliography

1992 American National Election Study. Available from National
   Election Studies, Center for Political Studies, University of
   Michigan. <http://www.umich.edu /~nes>. [9 March 1999]

1998 American National Election Study. Available from National
   Election Studies, Center for Political Studies, University of
   Michigan. <http://www.umich.edu /~nes>. [9 March 1999]

Almond, Gabriel A. and Sidney Verba. 1965. *The Civic Culture.*
   Boston: Little, Brown.

American Heritage Foundation. 1948. *Good citizen : the rights and
   duties of an American.* New York: American Heritage
   Foundation.

Auster, Lawrence. 1995. Them vs. Unz; special letters section. *Policy
   Review.* 71 (Winter) 88.

Bellah, Robert. 1975. *The Broken Covenant: American Civil Religion
   in Time of Trial.* New York: Seabury Press.

Bergquist, James M. 1992. German-Americans. In *Multiculturalism in
   the United States*, eds. John D. Buenker and Lorman A.
   Ratner, 53-76 . New York: Greenwood Press.

Bowman, Karlyn H. 2004. *America After 9/11: Public Opinion on The War on Terrorism, The War with Iraq, and America's Place in the World*, AEI Studies in Public Opinion, Papers and Studies, AEI Online, American Enterprise Institute, Washington D.C.

Brewer, David J. 1902. *American Citizenship.* New Haven, Conn.: Yale University Press.

Broome, Edwin C., Edwin W. Adams. 1926. *Conduct and Citizenship.* New York: The MacMillan Company.

Bridges, Horace J. 1919. *On Becoming an American.* Boston: Marshall Jones Company.

Briggs, Asa. 1966. *Saxons, Normans and Victorians.* London: London Historical Association.

Brimelow, Peter. 1995. *Alien Nation: Common Sense about America's Immigration Disaster.* New York: Random House.

Brubaker, Rogers, 1993. Migrants into citizens? Traditions of nationhood and politics of citizenship in france and Germany. In *Sociology and the Public Agenda*, ed. William Julius Wilson, 73-96. Newbury Park, Calif.: Sage.

Buenker, John D., and Lorman A. Ratner. 1992. *Multiculturalism in the United States.* New York: Greenwood Press.

Bushnell, Horace. 1837. The true wealth or weal of nations. In *Representative Phi Beta Kappa Orations*, eds. Northup, Clark S., William C. Lane and John C. Schwab, 1-12. Boston: Houghton Mifflin Company. 1915.

The California Poll. 1988. Study 8801, Question 67, February. Available from the Institute for Research in the Social Science <http://www.irss.unc.edu/tempdocs/ 23:46:38:1.htm>. [8 August 2000].

Carlson, Robert A. 1987. *The Americanization Syndrome: A Quest for Conformity*. London: Croom Helm.

Chase, Harold W., Craig R. Ducat. 1979. *Constitutional Interpretation*. 2d ed. St. Paul, Minn.: West Publishing Co.

Chavez, Leo. 1997. Official English as nativist backlash. In *Immigrants Out!* ed. Juan F. Perea, 61-77. New York: New York University Press.

Citrin, Jack, Ernst B. Haas, Christopher Muste, and Beth Reingold. 1994. Is American Nationalism Changing? Implications for Foreign Policy. *International Studies Quarterly*. 38 (March) 1-31.

Clark, Dennis. 1992. Irish-Americans. In *Multiculturalism in the United States*, eds. John D. Buenker and Lorman A. Ratner, 53-76 . New York: Greenwood Press.

Cubberley, Ellwood P. 1909. *Changing Conceptions of Education*. Boston: Houghton Mifflin Co.

Dahl, Robert A. 1996. Is civic virtue a relevant ideal in a pluralist democracy? In *Diversity and Citizenship*, eds. Gary Jeffrey Jacobsohn and Susan Dunn, 1-16. Lanham, Md.: Rowman & Littlefield Publishers, Inc.

De Koven, Mrs. Reginald. 1923. *A Primer of Citizenship*. New York: E.P. Dutton & Company.

Dewey, John. 1916. Nationalizing Education. *Addresses and Proceedings of the Fifty-fourth Annual Meeting*. National Education Association of the United States. Washington, D.C.

D'innocenzo, Michael and Josef P. Sirefman. 1992. *Immigration and Ethnicity*. Westport, Conn.: Greenwood Press.

Eastland, Terry and William J. Bennett. 1979. *Counting by Race :
    Equality from the Founding Fathers to Bakke and Weber.*
    New York: Basic Books.

Etzioni, Amitai. 1993. *The Spirit of Community.* New York: Crown
    Publisher, Inc.

Espenshade, Thomas J. and Katherine Hempstead. 1996.
    Contemporary American attitudes toward U.S. immigration.
    International Migration Review. 30 (Summer) 535-70.

Fuchs, Lawrence H. 1990. *The American Kaleidoscope.* London:
    Wesleyan University Press.

Fulford, James. 2004. *Minding the 'Golden Door:' Toward a
    Restrictionism that can Succeed.* [online] available through
    VDARE.com.

Gans, Herbert. 1979. Symbolic ethnicity: the future of ethnic groups
    and cultures in America. *Ethnic and Racial Studies*, 2/1: 1-20.

Garza, Rodolfo O. de la. 1996. Will the real American please stand
    up: anglo and Mexican-American support of core American
    political values. *American Journal of Political Science.* 40:2
    (May): 335-51.

Gates, Henry Louis Jr. 1995. Back and James Brown: on honoring
    Blackness. *The American Enterprise.* 6 (Sept./Oct): 49.

General Social Survey. 1994. Available at
    <http://www.icpsr.umich.edu/GSS/>. [9 March 1999]

Glazer, Nathan. 1996. Reflections on citizenship and diversity. In
    Diversity and Citizenship, eds. Gary Jeffrey Jacobsohn and
    Susan Dunn, 85-100. Lanham, Md.: Rowman & Littlefield
    Publishers, Inc.

Gleason, Philip. 1984. Pluralism and assimilation: a conceptual history. In *Linguistic Minorities: Policies and Pluralism*, ed. John Edwards, 221-257. New York: Academic Press.

Glendon, Mary Ann. 1991. *Rights Talk*. New York: The Free Press.

Gordon, Milton M. 1964. *Assimilation in American Life: The Role of Race, Religion, and National Origins*. New York: Oxford University Press.

Grund, Francis Joseph. 1837. *The Americans in Their Moral, Social, and Political Relations*. Boston: March, Capen and Lyon.

Hardy-Fanta, Carol. 1993. *Latina Politics, Latino Politics: Gender, Culture, and Political Participation in Boston*. Philadelphia: Temple University Press.

Hartman, Edward George. 1967. *The Movement to Americanize the Immigrant*. New York: AMS Press, Inc. Original Edition, New York: Columbia University Press, 1948.

Louis Harris and Associates Polls. 1992. Study S921204. Available at <http://www.irss.unc.edu/tempdocs/ 20:26:45:1.htm>. [9 May 1999]

Harrington, M. 1980. Loyalty: Dual and Divided. In *The Harvard Encyclopedia of American Ethnic Groups*. Ed. Stephan Thernstrom, 676-86. Cambridge, Mass.: Harvard University Press.

Hepner, Walter R., and Frances K. Hepner. 1924. *The Good Citizen*. Boston: Houghton Mifflin Company.

Herberg, Will. 1955. *Protestant-Catholic-Jew*. Garden City, New York: Doubleday and Company, Inc.

Horsman, Reginald 1981. *Race and Manifest Destiny*. Cambridge, Mass.: Harvard University Press.

Huntington, Samuel P. 1981. *American Politics: The Promise of Disharmony.* Cambridge, Mass.: Belknap Press.

Jacobsohn, Gary Jeffrey and Susan Dunn. 1996. *Diversity and Citizenship.* Lanham, Md.: Rowman & Littlefield Publishers, Inc.

Janoski, Thomas. 2000. *Citizenship and Civil Society.* New York: Cambridge University Press,

Janowitz, Morris. 1980. Observations on the sociology of citizenship: obligations and rights. *Social Forces,* 59:1 (September): 1-24.

Jefferson, Thomas. 1984. *Writings.* Compiled by Peterson, Merrill D. New York: Viking Press.

Kallen, Horace. 1924. *Culture and Democracy in the United States.* New York: Boni and Liveright.

Keefe, Susan E., and Amado M. Padilla. 1987. *Chicano Ethnicity.* Albuquerque: University of New Mexico Press.

Kettner, James H. 1978. *The Development of American Citizenship, 1608-1870.* Chapel Hill: University of North Carolina Press.

Kolasky, Bob. 1997. Issue of the week: a 'Nation of Immigrants.' Available from Intellectual Capital.Com at <http://www.IntellectualCapital.com>. [6 February 1997].

Kymlicka, Will, and Wayne Norman. 1994. Return of the Citizen: A Survey of Recent Work on Citizenship Theory. *Ethics.* 104 (January): 352-381. Chicago.: University of Chicago Press.

Kymlicka, Will. 1995. *Multicultural Citizenship.* New York: Oxford University Press Inc.

Lieberson, Stanley. 1985. Unhyphenated whites in the United States. *Ethnic and Racial Studies.* 8 (January) 159-80.

Lincoln, Abraham. 1947. *The Lincoln Reader.* Edited by Paul M.
Angle. New Brunswick, Conn.: Rutgers University Press.

Marshall, T.H. 1973. *Class, Citizenship and Social Development.*
Westport, Conn.: Greenwood Press.

Morgan, David L., and Richard A. Krueger. 1998. *The Focus Group
Kit.* Thousand Oaks, Calif.: Sage Publications, Inc.

Muller, Thomas. 1997. Nativism in the mid-1990's. In *Immigrants
Out!*, ed. Juan F. Perea, 105-18. New York: New York
University Press.

Nelson, Candace, and Marta Tienda. 1985. Structuring of Hispanic
ethnicity: Historical and contemporary perspectives. *Ethnic
and Racial Studies*, 8 (Jan): pp 49-74.

Novak, Michael. 1973. *The Rise of the Unmeltable Ethnics.* New
York: The Macmillan Company.

Pachon, Harry, and Louis DeSipio. 1994. *New Americans by Choice.*
Boulder, Colo.: Westview Press.

Perea, Juan F. ed. 1997. *Immigrants Out!* New York: New York
University Press.

Petersen, William. 1997. *Ethnicity Counts.* New Brunswick, Conn.:
Transaction Publishers.

Pinkerton, John. 1787. *A Dissertation on the Origin and Progress of
the Scythians or Goths. Being an introduction to the ancient
and modern history of Europe.* London: G. Nicol.

*Population Projections for States by Age, Sex, Race, and Hispanic
Origin: 1995 to 2025*, Census Bureau PPL-47, October, 1996.

Portes, Alejandro, and Rubén G. Rumbaut. 1990. *Immigrant America.*
Berkeley: University of California Press.

Portes, Alejandro, and Min Zhou. 1993. The New Second Generation: Segmented Assimilation and Its Variants. *The Annals of the American Academy of Political and Social Sciences*, 530 (November): 74-96.

Portes, Alejandro, and Min Zhou. 1994. Should Immigrants Assimilate. *The Public Interest*, 116 (Summer): 18-33.

Putnam, Robert D. 1995. Bowling alone: America's declining social capital. *Journal of Democracy*, 6:1 (January): 65-78

Putnam, Robert D. 2000. *Bowling Alone*. New York: Simon & Schuster.

Reynolds, John F. Reynolds. 1988. *Testing Democracy: Electoral Behavior and Progressive Reform in New Jersey, 1880-1920.* Chapel Hill, N.C.: University of North Carolina Press.

Roberts, Kenneth L. 1922. *Why Europe Leaves Home*. London: T. Fisher Unwin, Ltd.

Rossiter, Clinton. ed. 1961. *The Federalist Papers*. New York: Penguin Inc.

Schlesinger, Arthur Meier. 1992. *The Disuniting of America*. New York: W.W. Norton

Sellers, James. 1970. *Public Ethics : American Morals and Manners*. New York: Harper & Row.

Shklar, Judith N. 1991. *American Citizenship, The Quest for Inclusion*. Cambridge Mass.: Harvard University Press.

Smith, Rogers M. 1988. The "American Creed" and American identity: the limits of liberal citizenship in the United States. *The Western Political Quarterly*. 41 (June): 225-51.

-------- 1997. *Civic Ideals*. New Haven, Conn.: Yale University Press.

Smith, Tom W. 1980. Ethnic measurement and identification.
   Ethnicity. 7 (March) 78-95.

Sons of the American Revolution. 1911. *Official Bulletin*. 2 (Oct.
   1911): 2.

Thompson, Michael, Richard Ellis, and Aaron Wildavsky. 1990.
   Cultural Theory. Boulder, Colo.: Westview Press.

Tocqueville, Alexis de. 1984. *Democracy in America*. Edited by
   Richard D. Heffner. New York: Mentor.

Tilly, Louise A. and Patricia Gurin, eds. 1990. *Women, Politics, and
   Change*. New York: Russell Sage Foundation.

UCLA Academic Technology Services. 2000. *SPSS Frequently Asked
   Questions B What does Cronbach's Alpha Mean?* Available
   [Online] <www.ats.ucla.edu/stat/spss/ faq/alpha.html>. [16
   January 2001].

Ungar, Sanford. 1995. *Fresh Blood: The New American Immigrants*.
   New York : Simon & Schuster.

U. S. Commission on Immigration Reform. 1995. *Legal Immigration:
   Setting Priorities*. Washington, D.C.: GPO.

U.S. Congress. House. 1790. 1st Cong., 2d sess. *Annals of Congress*
   1 (3-4 February).

U.S. Congress. House. 1794. 3rd Cong., 2d sess. *Annals of Congress*
   4 (22 December).

U.S. Congress. Senate. 1845. 28th Cong., 2d sess. *Congressional
   Globe* 85 Appendix (21-22 February).

U.S. Congress. Senate. 1848. 30th Cong., 1st sess. *Congressional
   Globe* 89 (2 January).

U.S. Congress. Senate. 1896. 54th Cong., 1st sess. *Congressional Record.* 28, pt. 3, (16 March).

U.S. Congress. Senate. Committee on the Judiciary, Subcommittee on Immigration and Refugee Policy. 1981. *The Final Report and Recommendations of the Select Commission on Immigration and Refugee Policy.* Washington, D.C.: GPO.

U.S. Census Bureau, Census 2000 Brief, *Overview of Race and Hispanic Origin*, by Elizabeth M. Grieco, and Rachel C. Cassidy. Washington, DC, 2001.

-------- Current Population Reports, Series P20-539. *The Foreign-Born Population in the United States: March 2002*, by Dianne Schmidley. Washington, D.C. 2003.

-------- Current Population Reports, Series P23-206. *Profile of the Foreign-Born Population in the United States: 2000*, by Dianne Schmidley. Washington, DC. 2001.

Walzer, Michael. 1990. What Does it Mean to be an American? *Social Research.* 57 (Fall): 591-614.

Waters, Mary C. 1990. *Ethnic Options.* Berkeley: University of California Press.

Wilkinson, J. Harvie III. 1997. *One Nation Indivisible.* Reading, Mass.: Addison-Wesley Publishing Company, Inc.

Wrinkle, Robert D., Joseph Stewart, Jr., J.L. Polinard, Kenneth J. Meier, John R. Arvizu. 1996. Ethnicity and Nonelectoral Political Participation. *Hispanic Journal of Behavioral Sciences*, 18:2 (May): 142-153.

Index

Almond 39, 65, 147
American Heritage Foundation
    72, 147
Americans are Not Truly a
    People 40
Anglo 1, 19, 21, 22, 23, 24, 28,
    34, 35, 36, 38, 40, 43, 52,
    56, 60, 117, 118, 130, 139
Anglo-Americans 19
Ascriptive Criteria 29, 50, 51
Auster 14, 147
backward elimination process
    95, 96, 98
belief in the American system
    of government viii, 62, 79,
    81, 82, 87, 90, 92, 100, 131,
    143, 145
Bergquist 26, 52, 147
Brewer 16, 23, 27, 31, 58, 66,
    142, 148
Bridges 26, 60, 61, 62, 148
Briggs 19, 148
Brimelow 25, 28, 148
Broome 72, 148
Brown v. Board of Education
    46, 51
Buckley 71
Bushnell 20, 148

California Poll 24, 74, 148
Carlson 18, 25, 28, 42, 63, 149
Chavez 4, 5, 149
Chinese Exclusion Case 31
Citrin 74, 149
Clark 36, 148, 149
Congress 21, 29, 30, 31, 46,
    47, 48, 49, 50, 66, 142, 155
Cubberley 22, 140, 149
cultural factors 7, 25
culture 4, 14, 16, 17, 19, 21,
    25, 26, 27, 28, 29, 34, 35,
    37, 38, 39, 40, 41, 42, 52,
    53, 54, 55, 56, 57, 58, 59,
    60, 62, 64, 65, 66, 79, 99,
    106, 115, 116, 117, 130,
    132, 133, 135, 138, 139,
    140, 145
Dahl 27, 53, 67, 135, 142, 149
De Koven 72, 149
Dewey 59, 149
Dred Scott 29, 30, 50, 130
English only 76
Espenshade and Hempstead
    13
ethnicity and race 17, 18, 21,
    25, 33, 34, 37, 42, 52
Ethnocentric 38

Etzioni 71, 150
Factor Analysis 91
Focus Group Organization 104
Focus Group Participant
    Selection Criteria 105
Focus Group Results 114, 144
Fourteenth Amendment 31, 42,
    43, 44, 45, 48, 79, 140, 141
Franklin 18, 36, 39, 54, 55
Fuchs 18, 39, 57, 58, 64, 65,
    150
Gallup poll 14
Gates 59, 150
General Social Survey 14, 74,
    76, 77, 78, 139, 140, 143,
    150
Glazer 16, 25, 74, 150
Gleason 27, 151
Glendon 71, 151
Gordon 19, 26, 38, 56, 57, 58,
    59, 74, 151
Grovey 32, 33, 42, 44, 50
Grund 63, 64, 151
GSS 74, 75, 76, 77, 78, 150
Hardy-Fanta 69, 151
Harlan 32, 140
Harrington 40, 52, 53, 65, 151
Harris 14, 151
Hartman 21, 57, 73, 151
Hepners 72
Herberg 24, 151
Hirabayashi 33, 41, 51
Hirabayashi v. United States
    33
Hispanics 4, 28, 41, 105, 144
Horsman 17, 18, 20, 138, 151,
    161
Huntington 7, 8, 20, 25, 54,
    56, 61, 62, 63, 65, 105, 139,
    144, 152

Interview Questions 111
Jacobsohn 39, 55, 149, 150,
    152
Jacobsohn, Jeffery, and Dunn
    39
Janoski 68, 72, 152
Janowitz 16, 69, 142, 152
Jefferson 19, 152
Jones v. Alfred H. Mayer Co.
    48, 51
Kallen 38, 39, 42, 58, 59, 152
Katzenbach v. Morgan 47, 51
Kennedy 36
Kluckhohn 56
Kolasky 13, 152
Korematsu 33, 41, 51, 141
Kymlicka 13, 28, 40, 60, 70,
    152
language 9, 18, 21, 26, 30, 40,
    54, 57, 59, 60, 62, 73, 74,
    76, 77, 78, 85, 86, 87, 90,
    99, 100, 107, 109, 115, 117,
    131, 139, 143
Language of the Focus Groups
    107
learning English viii, 62, 68,
    73, 80, 81, 82, 130, 143
Learning English 73, 85
Lincoln 21, 64, 153
Lipset 56
Lodge 30
Los Angeles Times 24
Loving v. Virginia 47, 51
Loyalty 52, 53, 151
Mallary 73
Marshall 68, 69, 71, 148, 153
McLaurin v. Oklahoma State
    Regents 45
Missouri ex rel Gaines v.
    Canada 45

model 7, 9, 83, 93, 95, 96, 98, 99
mongrelization 23
Morgan 104, 153
Muller 4, 153
National Election Study 74, 147
National Latino Immigrant Survey 3
NBC News, Wall Street Journal survey 14
NES 74, 76, 77, 78
Nixon v. Condon 44
NLIS viii, 3, 5, 7, 8, 9, 10, 14, 73, 80, 81, 82, 83, 84, 85, 86, 87, 88, 89, 90, 92, 99, 100, 101, 102, 103, 104, 105, 107, 109, 110, 111, 129, 130, 131, 132, 134, 141, 144
Novak 56, 57, 153
Pachon and DeSipio vii, 3
Participant Demographics 109
Participation in the political process 84
participation in the political/electoral process viii, 68, 79, 81, 82, 130, 143
participation in voluntary associations 68, 70
Participation in Voluntary Associations 69
participation in voluntary organizations viii, 79, 82, 83
Petersen 28, 63, 153
Ping v. U.S 31
Pinkerton 18, 153

Plessy 31, 42, 45, 46, 50, 130, 140
political participation 9, 29, 56, 69, 84, 87, 121, 126, 133, 142
Portes and Rumbaut 13
Putnam 70, 100, 132, 142, 154
Roberts 23, 140, 142, 154
Schlesinger 27, 34, 35, 36, 39, 154
Sedgewick 66
Shelley v. Kraemer 44, 51
Shklar 70, 154
Simpson 28
Sipuel v. Oklahoma 45
Smith 16, 17, 29, 31, 32, 33, 34, 36, 38, 50, 59, 99, 154, 155
Smith v. Allwright 44
South Carolina v. Katzenbach 72
Speaking English 75, 77, 78
Strauder 42, 44, 50, 140
Strauder v. West Virginia 42, 50
Summary of Legal Cases 49
Supreme Court vii, 8, 15, 29, 30, 31, 34, 36, 37, 42, 43, 44, 46, 47, 48, 49, 60, 72, 79, 98, 130, 134, 140
Sweatt v. Painter 45
Taney 29
Tape Recording the Focus Groups 108
The Civil Rights Cases 30, 42, 50
The Ku Klux Cases 72
Thompson 56, 155
Tilly and Gurin 69

Tocqueville 64, 69, 70, 132, 155
U.S. Congress 20, 28, 30, 66, 155, 156
Ungar 57, 155
vote 33, 34, 47, 72, 74, 84, 85, 88, 118, 122, 127, 140
Walzer 35, 40, 63, 156
Warren 46, 48, 51

Waters 22, 59, 156
What Is An American 130
Wildavsky 56, 155
Wilkinson 13, 28, 52, 130, 138, 156
Wilson 25, 52, 65, 148
Wrinkle 73, 156
Yick Wo v. Hopkins 43, 50, 141